Maya Investigations
volume 1

A Collection of Research Papers
concerning the Maya

Janice Van Cleve

Library of Congress Control Number: pending

ISBN-13: 9781503194458
ISBN-10: 1503194450

Cover illustration: Throne room scene from a Maya vase rollout by Justin Kerr, no. 694. Royalty was paid for use of this illustration.

Title page illustration: Central medallion from the famous Copan Peccary Skull. Drawing by Barbara Fash.

This book was printed in the United States of America.

To order additional copies of this book, go to www.CreateSpace.com/5097058. Copies may also be ordered from Amazon at www.amazon.com or from your local book seller.

Additional Books by the author:

Eighteen Rabbit – The Intimate Life and Tragic
Death of a Maya God-King (2006)

The Founder – The Life of Yax Kuk Mo, Mover
and Shaker in the Maya World (2010)

America: Course Correction (2011)

Dandelion (2013)

Sound and Summits (2014)

Table of Contents

Preface

Over the years I have produced a quantity of articles on the Maya, partly in preparation for the biographies of Eighteen Rabbit and Yax Kuk Mo. Along the way, my curiosity led me to other topics worthy of exploration. These articles appeared from time to time on a website and were taken down when I put up a new one.

The purpose of these volumes is to capture in print and make permanently available these articles and research papers. Volume 1 contains a collection of non-biographical subjects. Volume 2 will contain the background research for a number of high ranking Maya individuals.

My focus is centered on Copan, but its connection to Tikal – particularly to the Entrada of 378 and to the ongoing alliance between the two cities – caused me to focus on that center and the larger political framework of the Maya world as well.

By great good fortune I was able to secure a complete set of the Copan Notes published by Linda Schele et. al. which delve into details not available elsewhere. I am grateful for these and I have included in this volume a catalog of all 121 Copan Notes.

Janice Van Cleve, 2014

OBSERVATIONS ON THE MAYA

The following story is the result of my first visit to the Maya lands in March 2000 and finally put down in writing in 2008. The cruise was booked as the "Maya Equinox Cruise", scheduled to culminate in witnessing the "descent of the snake" on El Castillo in Chichen Itza on March 21. Anthony Aventi, noted archeoastronomer, was our lecturer on the trip.

The imposing memorials of the ancient Maya dramatically overthrew my images of this mysterious civilization. Before I visited this cultural grail of Mesoamerica, I had harbored visions of dank jungles, large snakes, and brooding temples strangled in vines. I had thoughts of a vanished race, an advanced people with science, astronomy, and peaceful government who took their secrets with them to the grave. Some people have even proposed that Egyptians, Phoenicians, or even space aliens ignited the Maya civilization. All of these images were challenged in the grounded presence of hewn stone and graven figures. I found the reality even more fascinating than imagination.

The cruise was booked as an educational adventure that took us to Honduras, Guatemala, Belize, and Yucatan. On board we received books, lectures, and films about the sights we were about to visit. At each port, we were bussed inland to the famous lost cities of Maya history: Copan, Quirigua, Tikal, Coba, and Chichen Itza. There are literally hundreds of other sites in the region, many of them still unmapped and or only partially excavated. These five are among the most famous. They sketch the skeleton of a story, a story that begins before the Age of Alexander of Macedonia and ends with the belching cannons of Spanish conquistadors.

Undoubtedly some of my former impressions came from the stores of travel writer John Stephens and his fellow adventurer, architect Frederick Catherwood. I had read their books and seen their illustrations. They arrived in Central America in 1839 and spent the next ten months exploring the Maya sites. Stephens' prose was as colorful and intense as Catherwood's highly detailed etchings. He writes:

"Who were the people that built this city?. . . The place where we were sitting, was it a citadel from which an unknown people had sounded the trumpet of war? or a temple for the worship of God in peace?. . . All was mystery, dark, impenetrable mystery. . . In Egypt the colossal skeletons of gigantic temples stand in unwatered sands in all the nakedness of desolation; but here an immense forest shrouds the ruins, hiding them from sight, heightening the impression and moral effect, and giving an intensity and almost wildness to the interest . . . Here were the remains of a cultivated, polished people, who had passed through all the stages incidental to the rise and fall of nations, reached their golden age and perished, entirely unknown." (Stephens, "Incidents of Travel in the Yucatan, 1843)

Much scientific archeological work has been done since Stephens wrote that text. Many of the inscriptions of the Maya have been deciphered and many cities have been explored and opened to the public. Some of the forest has been cleared and a large number of the major structures have been partially restored. New technologies and radars are discovering more sites every day. Actual photographs have circulated in journals, books, and travel brochures. Yet no representation or explanation can substitute for first hand experience of these marvelous remains of the Maya civilization.

Copan was the first place I visited. Copan is nestled in a broad valley 2000 ft. up in the western mountains of Honduras. The steep hillsides are home to pine trees and coffee plantings. Farms and cattle pastures dot the valley floor. The ruins of the central core of the ancient city loom above the Copan river. In fact, the river had to be diverted because it was undermining the ruins and would have eventually washed them away.

While most of the area around the site has been cleared, it is easy to see from inside the great plaza how aggressively the vegetation attempts to claim every foot of space. Unless checked, trees will sprout from crack and crevice; roots and vines will literally tear the stone buildings apart. Surveys indicate that in the city's heyday there were no trees here, or anywhere in the valley. In fact, the stripping of vegetation for fuel and stucco plaster is speculated to be the reason for the massive erosion and crop failure that eventually caused the decline and fall of Copan sometime in the 10th Century. So much for my image of dank jungles!

Nor did the Maya take their secrets with them to the grave. Stelae, large carved monoliths in the plazas before the temples, display images of the rulers on the front while on the sides or at least on the back are displayed inscriptions listing their names, dates, lineage, and accomplishments. Formerly disregarded as mere religious totems, these monuments are history books in stone. They detail the succession of the sixteen rulers of Copan from its conquest by Yax Kuk Mo in 427 to the death of Yax Pac sometime around 820. They tell of a small ruling elite who dominated their people by force and religious magic and who gave their own blood in sacrificial rites for the fertility of the land.

Sometimes more than their own blood offering was needed and rulers led their bodyguards in raids on neighboring towns to capture other nobles for heart rending (pardon the pun!) sacrifices on the high altars. Eighteen Rabbit, 13th ruler of Copan from 695 to 738, was caught in one such raid by Cauac Sky, ruler of Quirigua, in what is today Guatemala. He was tortured and finally beheaded on May 3, 738. The history is elaborately described on monuments erected in Quirigua. So much for peaceful government!

The existence of such a precise, detailed historical record, as well as monumental architecture, advanced mathematics, and astronomy has led some writers to theorize that Egyptians or aliens must have visited the Maya and showed them how to do these things. "Rubbish!", explained our Honduran guide with a flourish of national pride. "That is so much Eurocentric egotism. Why can't they credit my people with the invention of these things on their own?" Indeed, the Maya did invent a calendar accurate to within 23 seconds per year. They also invented the use of zero (not introduced into Europe until the 10th Century by Arabs via Spain) and of positional mathematics. Positional mathematics is what we use today to express any size number with only 10 characters. The Roman method, by contrast, is much more clumsy as any student who has tried to perform simple multiplication using Roman numerals can attest.

Not only have the secrets of the Maya remained, but so have the people. Over seven million people in Chiapas, Yucatan, Honduras, Belize, Salvador, and Guatemala trace their ancestry to the Maya and still speak Mayan dialects. The faces of the people I met at the vending stalls along our way bore the same features as I saw on the stelae. Unfortunately today's Maya often occupy the lowest social and economic strata in nation states imposed by outsiders. Western influence and the Catholic Church have overlaid the society and economy of the Maya people with an oppressive veneer. Yet in many places the the people still pursue the customs and traditions by which they remember their past – and the stones also remember.

The stones tell of an ancient people who used no metal, no beasts of burden, and no wheels. Yet they moved mountains of rock and earth – and built their own mountains – my sheer human will and strength alone. It was a most difficult idea for me to reconcile the notion of a Stone Age culture with the obvious spectacular advances the Maya made in other areas. The contrast illustrates that the Sumerian-Egyptian-Greek-Roman model is not the only possible model in which a civilization may evolve.

The buildings at Copan enclose very little interior space. The Maya never learned how to construct the true arch. Instead they extended stones out from the walls like stacked dominos to create narrow vaulted ceilings called corbelled arches. Corbelled arches demand massive walls to bear their weight. These walls were built on all sides of stone blocks stacked and mortared in place and then filled with rubble and mud. This is not the fine fitted masonry of the Incas or of the Greeks. No wonder tree roots found invasion easy! Yet the exterior surfaces of the buildings were elaborately decorated with masks of gods and panels of hieroglyphic writing. Often the exteriors were also embellished with stucco sculptures and painted. Traces of the original red, blue, green and yellow pigments still cling to the carvings. The reconstruction of the Rosalila temple in the Sculpural Museum at Copan demonstrates the elaborate ornamentation with which the Maya decorated their temples. What an impression these huge, colored structures would have made looming over suburb and field and visible for miles!

Archeologists have found traces of buildings spreading far out from the central complex in all directions. These suburbs included upper class houses among clusters of thatched huts in irregular patterns, more like medieval European cities than the orderly blocks of Teotihuacan or Tenochtitilan to the northwest in central Mexico. It is estimated that Copan was home to 27,000 people at its height.

I gained a new image of the Maya from observations at this one site. I can see a sprawling urban city state with a large ceremonial and governmental complex at its center. Smoke from cooking fires and incense offerings wisp up above the thatched roofs and painted stone temples. Dominating rulers, who command loyalty and worship, are themselves trapped between a life of wealth and power and their duty to provide expensive blood (theirs, or the blood of other victims) to their thirsty gods. The government appears static, maintaining itself by using science to predict astronomical phenomena and weather and then dramatizing the results in magic and ritual to awe the populace.

I can see an economy that is also static, rooted in a simple, undiversified agrarian pattern that consumes surrounding forests until the land can sustain no more. Based on measurements in the city suburbs, experts think that the population reached a critical mass in the late 8th Century (when Charlemagne was born). Eroding soil and failing crops confronted the leadership, which at the same time was struggling to regain its prestige after Eighteen Rabbit was executed. The pressures were too much, the magic of the ruling elite was broken, and the people's confidence in the leaders was lost. The elite appear to have died off or were killed and the city was not maintained. By 900, most of the core was abandoned and by 1200 even the remaining squatters surrendered the magnificent structures of Copan to the jungle.

Quirigua was our next stop. It is a small imitation of Copan located across the hills from the latter on the Motagua River in Guatemala. It has a great plaza, a ballcourt, and acropolis and the tallest stelae in the Maya world. It was a trade center for jade, obsidian, and other goods between Kaminaljuju and what is now Belize. Much of the elaborate architecture dates from the reign of Cauac Sky, who must have nursed a deep inferiority complex vis a vis his rival and former master, Eighteen Rabbit. He bragged about his capture and execution of the latter several times on his monuments and even copied Copan stela J's mat pattern for his own stela H.

Quirigua is located on a flood plain and the plaza is often ankle deep in water. The place is surrounded today by banana plantations. Having already become impressed by Eighteen Rabbit, I have to admit that my own feelings about Cauac Sky and his city were less positive.

Tikal came closer to my original assumptions. Concealed deep in the thickest jungles of northern Guatemala, this huge Maya city evokes awe and mystery at every turn. Over 3500 buildings have been discovered, blanketing an area over six square miles. Temples burst through the dense trees to heights of 228 feet. Government and religious centers cover whole city blocks. Paved streets connect major ceremonial and functional centers. Excavations of hundreds of tombs at Tikal and of earlier structures buried beneath later ones, indicate a continuous period of construction in the city from roughly the time of Hannibal to the time of the Vikings (200 BCE to 900 CE).

Too bad our tour group had only three hours in this magnificent city. Too bad I did not have detailed guidebooks, or even a map, to tell me about the wonders that surrounded me on every side. Nevertheless, I resolved to take in as much as I could through my physical senses, climbing, probing, exploring, and taking the feel and placement of the stones into my cellular memory. Looking back now, when I am able to fill in the picture with data from text books, I recall the sense of the rooms and courtyards. It is still excitingly vivid.

Tikal sets the standard for the Maya civilization in most peoples' imaginations. Not quite as ornate and detailed as Copan, nor yet as bold and solid as Chichen Itza, Tikal by its size and political dominance represents the height of Maya culture. Stelae, with their round stone altars before them, proclaim the deeds and succession of Tikal's rulers. One king, Jaguar Paw, asserts his independence from El Mirador in a stela erected in 292 and by 358, Tikal's emblem glyph (coat of arms) appears on the stelae of other cities in the area, indicating its overlordship. By 470 Tikal had extended its influence all the way to Copan in the east and to Palenque in the west. I later learned that Tikal was not alone in power. Calakmul to the north was a major rival and the other Maya city states appear to have been very flexible in their loyalties.

Tikal accelerated my changing impressions of the Maya. The basis of its power and reach of influence was not agriculture or religion or military dominance. Tikal was based on trade and strategic alliances. The city is located on the middle ground between the rivers that flow to the

Gulf of Mexico and those that flow to the Caribbean. Imports and exports, traveling by canoe, found their central market in Tikal and the power elite skimmed the tributes to finance their rule. The Maya were evidently a very mercantile people, with economic connections and a Weltanschauung or "world view" that extended far beyond their cultural borders.

How far did their view extend? That was even more surprising! Tikal was connected to Kaminaljuyu (now Guatemala City far to the south) and to Teotihuacan (north of Mexico City!). I had previously believed that the Maya were an isolated race, a self contained civilization. I had not imagined a directed and intentional influence by Central Mexico on these people. Yet, it appears that Teotihuacan, that huge Mexican city dominated by the famous Temple of the Sun, was the center of a mercantile and military empire that reached deep into Maya country. Indeed, a general named Siyaj Kak lead a Teotihuacan army into the Maya lands and captured Tikal in 378 CE. Carvings tell of colonies of Teotihuacano merchants and soldiers in Maya cities. One of Tikal's greatest rulers, Stormy Sky, is portrayed on stela 31 in traditional Maya dress, but he is flanked on either side by images of his father dressed in Teotihuacan military fashion with Teotihuacano weapons and helmets.

Could the invaders have been mercenaries? The stelae tell a tangled tale. Two were erected in 527 and only one in 557. Then nothing until 692. Jaguar Paw Skull claims in 527 to be the 14th ruler of Tikal, yet Double Bird claims in 557 to be the 21st ruler and he states he gained power in 537. Seven rulers in only 10 years? Sounds like coups, palace intrigue, and warring factions to me. These are ripe conditions for mercenaries.

Inscriptions at Caracol, a huge Maya city east of Tikal, fill the gap. They tell of the defeat of Double Bird in 562 and his replacement by Animal Skull, who is not his son. Could it be that the losers of a power play in Tikal went to Caracol and got help to overthrow their rivals in Tikal? Maybe. Inscriptions at Dos Pilas, a small city south of Tikal, record a ruler named Flint Sky who fled there in 645 (he may have been part of Double Bird's faction) and rapidly consolidated his position through marriage and conquest. In 679 he returned to Tikal, captured Shield Skull, Animal Skull's son, and sacrificed him. Then, four years later, Shield Skull's son, Jasaw Chan, overthrew Flint Sky and led Tikal to a revival of its former power during his 50 year reign.

Of course, I did not personally read all this history from the stones. I saw the stones and picked up the history in books later. Why do I digress into history instead of sticking with the travelog? Precisely because it reveals a very complex, sophisticated, and turbulent society that sometimes seems to rival Greece and Rome or even recalls Machievelli's Renaissance Italy. I had to probe deeper. These rapid coups and counter coups could only be accomplished if there was excess wealth in many hands and mercenary troops available for hire. Teotihuacan was declining during the 6th Century and perhaps some of its imperial troops on the frontiers were unemployed.

The possibility of Mexican mercenaries in Maya country is backed by another piece of evidence: beards and facial hair. Most of the early Maya images show clean shaven men. Stelae and painted images in the 9th Century, however, show figures with long hair, moustaches and beards which is a Mexican style. One wood statue from Tabasco on the gulf coast shows a seated man with a fancy curled handlebar that would have made Wyatt Earp proud. A stela from Seibal south of Tikal dated 849 shows a ruler with full beard, moustache and long hair. One of Eighteen Rabbit's stela even shows him sporting a beard (although his other stelae do not). Some of these people may have been invaders/colonists, but others were locals adopting a fashion trend from outside.

Another surprising fact comes from the excavations at Tikal which are born out in Copan as well. Women also ruled. There are stelae bearing images of women, not only as wives but also as rulers. Smoke Monkey, 14th ruler of Copan, recorded on a stela how he acquired a princess from Palenque to shore up his authority after Eighteen Rabbit's untimely end. Temple 2 in Tikal was built for the wife of Jasaw Chan after his death, indicating her power in the succeeding government. Lady Six Sky is shown on a stela from Naranjo victorious in battle, standing upon her captured prisoner!

Tikal is also a beautiful wild natural park. Except for excavations, the Guatemalan government has preserved 576 square miles for this park. Trees up to 150 ft. tall shelter homes for monkeys, birds, snakes, wild pigs and jaguars. As I walked from Temple 4 to the Great Pyramid in the Mundo Perdido complex along a narrow trail, I heard rustling in the dry underbrush. It was more than one. There were a whole lot of them. They were on both sides of me. The second Jurassic Park movie flashed into my mind - with the vicious little raptors who left nothing but bones and binoculars in their wake. I was alone, in a jungle, in a far foreign country, and nobody knew where I was. Then I caught sight of one. Coatimundis! They appear like a cross between possums and raccoons. About forty-five of them surrounded me. They can be nasty little critters but somehow fur felt less threatening than reptilian scales. Gingerly, I evaded them and reached my goal unscathed.

Another movie recalled itself to me atop Temple 4. It was from this exact spot that George Lukas filmed the final scenes of the first Star Wars movie. The X-Wing fighters return to the rebel planet after exploding the Empire's Death Star They swoop out of the stratosphere over a jungle with temples protruding from the trees. That is Tikal! By curious coincidence, the destroyers of a fictional planetary empire land in the capital of an ancient real one.

The next city was Coba, a totally different experience. An old city, not far from Cancun, Coba was well established by the 7th Century and remained inhabited almost to the Spanish invasion. It dominated the eastern Yucatan in counterpoint to the Puuc centers of Uxmal and Sayil, which dominated the western half of the peninsula. The Yucatan peninsula is one big flat slab of limestone with no rivers and few lakes. Coba was fortunate to be able to claim five lakes within its domain. While surface water is rare, cenotes or sinkholes give access to underground water. The cenotes became the centers of cities like Chichen Itza.

While Coba exhibits the usual Maya features, such as stepped temples and ball courts, it possesses a feature totally new to Maya architecture: rounded pillars. These have been proposed as a Toltec influence from central Mexico. Pillars, and the now long vanished wooden beams that spanned them, were a new technological innovation. They permitted the Maya to enclose larger interior spaces with thinner walls than the old massive corbelled rooms of earlier times. Coba boasts over thirty stelae and at one time this sprawling city housed 50,000 people. Long paved roadways connect various parts of the metropolis and extend out across the surrounding countryside. These paved roads rival the famed Roman roads for durability and usefulness.

Coba's downfall was Chichen Itza. Located about 60 miles west of Coba, Chichen Itza is a large center in the middle of the northern Yucatan. It was a small town until the Itza tribe arrived in 987. The Itza were part of a general expansion of the Putan peoples who inhabited the gulf coast of Mexico, according to scholars. Archeological evidence suggests that these people were sea faring traders in large canoes. They apparently expanded from their coastal homeland into central Mexico and central Mayaland to fill the power vacuums created by the decline of Teotihuacan and Tikal. They apparently rerouted trade from the river highways to coastal routes, which is given as one of the reasons for Tikal's decline. They reminded me strongly of the "Sea Peoples" of the Eastern Mediterranean who upset Egypt, Greece, and Canaan in the 13th Century BCE. Some of these became the well known Philistines, whose behavior and role appears uncannily similar to the Itzas of 9th Century Yucatan!

The Itzas moved up the river highways into the heart of Maya country and captured Seibal in 830. They left by 900 and made their way north to Chichen Itza. Wall paintings in the Temple of Warriors at Chichen Itza indicate a merger between the Itza and the local upper class to form an oligarchy. During the 10th Century, the Itza extended their domination over most of Yucatan. They do not appear to have sacrificed the local rulers, but rather allowed them to remain in power as long as they paid tribute.

How the Toltecs got involved is very fuzzy. The Toltecs established themselves in Tula, 50 miles northwest of Mexico City about 900 CE under the leadership of Topiltzin who claimed the title Quetzalcoatl or "Feathered

Serpent." He was ousted by a military coup and fled to Yucatan with his soldiers. The Mayas record the arrival of one Kukulcan (which means "Feathered Serpent") in 987 at Chichen Itza. If this is the same person, he was practically 100 years old by then! The relationship between the Toltecs and the Itzas, who appear at Chichen Itza at the same time is not clear to me. Whatever is the case, Chichen Itza is full of Toltec architecture and carvings of feathered serpents. Another wall painting in the Temple of the Warriors shows peaceful Maya farmers at work with menacing Toltec warriors lurking in canoes off shore.

Chichen Itza is a large city with broad open spaces. The famous El Castillo pyramid temple looms over the central plaza with feathered serpents crowning the balustrade of the west stairway. At Spring Equinox, the setting sun catches the stepped angles of the southwest corner of the pyramid and casts their shadows on the balustrade. This produces a diamond zig zag effect that makes it look like the feathered serpent is descending from the temple on top to the square below. The same thing happens on the other side of the stairway at Autumn Equinox dawn. The phenomenon draws local and international tourists. About 500 people from our cruise ship disappeared in the crowd of approximately 50,000 people gathered for the event in the vast plaza.

The massive stark masonry of Toltec architecture is a sharp contrast to the delicate decorations of Copan and Tikal. The ball court is huge. The Caracol observatory is bulky. Great emphasis seems to have been placed on observations of Venus, the Maya/Toltec god of war. Most of the astrological alignments point to Venus. The Sacred Cenote west of the center is the famous Well of Sacrifice. Legends of young men and women weighted down with precious adornments being cast into the well from the temple platform at its edge, have been born out in dredgings of the bottom. The marketplace is studded with rounded columns whose roof timbers have long ago disappeared.

Most appealing to me, however, was the older, eastern section of town which preserves more of a northern Maya look. The buildings there huddle more closely together, their upper stories intricately decorated in patterns of stone which play with light and shadow. Rooms with corbelled ceilings honeycomb the structures and masks of gods leer from the corners.

Copan, Quirigua, Tikal, Coba, and Chichen Itza span the length of the Maya country and its history. They are but a few of the over 300 sites, large and small, that have been discovered by archeologists. I came away from them in awe and delight. It is not their architecture, their religion, or their science that intrigues me. It is their history. Here is a marvelous people shrouded in myth and mystery who left us names, dates, drama, and accomplishments stone carved in plain sight. They practically shout to us to read their past. I earned my Masters Degree in Medieval History. Stumbling upon so many records of untold stories is as exciting for me as it would be for Indiana Jones to find the gold of the Incas. History is gold and I am eager to tell the stories it describes.

The Maya written history, combined with their mathematics, calendrics, astronomy, sophisticated politics, art and architecture, and social organization blew away my assumptions of Stone Age classification. Maybe our Eurocentric yardstick is not an accurate measure of civilization after all. Perhaps if we learn to appreciate the Maya on their own terms instead of by our classifications we will not be so judgmental of other civilizations different from our own.

BEANS, BLOOD, AND BEER

Divination Among the Ancient Maya

In every culture and every age, humans have devised practices which they believed would enable them to learn things beyond the dimension of sensory experience and rational thought. Sometimes these practices entailed reading a supernatural interpretation into an otherwise ordinarily observed phenomenon. Other times these practices entailed altering the observer's state of consciousness. It is not surprising, therefore, to find such practices among the ancient Maya peoples of Mesoamerica.

The Maya civilization extended from the highlands of Mexico's Chiapas, through Yucatan, Guatemala, Belize, and El Salvador, to western Honduras. The Maya civilization rose to its classic expression between 250 – 900 CE. It must be noted, however, that Maya temples and writing existed before the classic period and that Maya city states were still engaged in civil wars in northern Yucatan when the Spanish arrived in 1524. Even today over seven million people in this region trace their ancestry to the Maya and many still speak Mayan dialects. Some still worship at the ancient sites and still practice the arts of divination that have been handed down over generations.

The Maya identified divination with the creation of the world. Through ritual and prayer, the diviner summons the gods of creation to come forth and manifest themselves in a tangible way.[1] Casting lots was for them not recreation but re-creation.

The Stars

Perhaps the most widely known divination method of the Maya is their achievements in astronomy and calendrics. Most cultures have attributed some auspices to the stars. From the Stonehenge solar calculator to the Magi of Babylon to the various European and Chinese zodiacs, people have "seen things" in the stars to which they imputed supernatural meaning. In the Americas, one theory for the purpose of the famous Nazca Lines in Peru is for astronomical sightings, although this has been debunked. Anthony Aveni and Michael Coe have proposed that they were walking paths like labyrinths for ceremonial rituals[2].

The Maya, however, took astronomy to heights (pardon the pun!) surpassing even the Arabs of their day. In particular they observed the passage of Venus, the war god. Its first appearance in the night sky was regarded as a favorable sign for initiating combat[3]. Lunar phases were measured to an accuracy close to that of our modern atomic clocks[4]. The positions of Venus, Orion, and the Milky Way were important enough to good fortune, that they were recorded on stone monuments marking the katuns, or 20 year cycles. The katun was considered the heartbeat of the universe and required human intervention to generate its next beat. Therefore an accurate calendar was absolutely necessary, not to inform the farmers when to plant, but to trigger the rituals that would continue the universe.

---

[1] Miller, p, 80.
[2] www.viewzone.com/nazcatheories.html.
[3] Milbrath, p. 193.
[4] Sharer, p. 565

Calendars

The Maya used three calendars simultaneously – the long count, the *haab,* and the *tzolkin.* The long count was a sequential count of days from a fixed point: August 11, 3114 BCE. What this date signified is not clear. The long count measured 5000 years to its last day on December 23, 2012 CE. Contrary to some modern writers, the Maya projected no eschealogical significance to the last date. For them, it simply means the resetting of the counter to begin the next 5000 year span. The long count system was not used for divination and in any event it fell into disuse after the end of the Classic Period and the rule of kings.

The *haab* calendar corresponds to our current 365 day calendar. It is basically an agricultural or solar calendar which informs farmers when to plant and when to harvest. David Stuart surmises that the word *haab* comes from the Mayan word for "rain" which is *ha*[5]. It may have referred to the rainy season and eventually come to mean the whole solar year.

The *tzolkin* calendar is a 260 day divination calculator based on the gestation period of a human baby[6]. Maya priests even today divine a person's fate based on the timing of their pregnancy and birth. Each day is associated with certain friendly and hostile deities who must be appeased or appealed to during a person's life[7]. Among the highland Maya, given names were fixed automatically as the *tzolkin.*

---

[5] Stuart, p. 108.
[6] Stuart, p. 155.
[7] Sharer, p. 231.

Beans

Casting the sacred red beans are still used today to make forecasts. In one form of bean casting called *mech*, a client poses a question to the shaman. The beans are cast: an odd number indicates a positive answer and an even number indicates a negative one[8]. Not all bean castings are the same. Linda Schele recounts a session in which she asked a question. The shaman asked her name and cast the beans three times, all the while chanting prayers and recounting the names of the days. Her friend went next and the shaman did it differently[9].

Beer, Tobacco, and Mushrooms

Alcohol has always been a part of Maya ritual practice, either as celebration or as a medium for altered states of consciousness. The Maya brewed a strong beer made from fermented maize[10]. Especially favored for ritual was another drink was made from fermented honey and the bark of the balche tree[11]. Bishop Landa recorded that alcoholic beverages were frequently drunk at ritual occasions and earlier paintings and figurines by Maya artisans do show drinking activities[12]. During my own participation in a Maximon ritual in Santiago Atitlan, Guatemala, we consumed several rounds of strong rum as part of the ceremony. Evan Vogt's classic study of the

---

[8] Sharer, p. 483.
[9] Schele, Maya Cosmos p. 227.
[10] Teotihuacanos used fermented agave (pulque) which also may have found its way into Maya practice. Proceedings of the National Academy of Sciences, September 2014 issue.
[11] Sharer, p.483.
[12] Landa, p. 57.

Zinacantecos describes the use of liquor at most of the important holiday celebrations[13]

Tobacco was used for pleasure or to create hallucinatory effects. Stronger than modern domestic tobaccos, the leaves of wild tobacco were rolled into cigars or chopped up for use in pipes. Tobacco was also consumed as snuff. The crushed leaves were combined with lime in a ratio of ten to one to increase the potency of the nicotine. The effect was intoxicating[14].

Mushrooms were also used for their psychotropic effects. In the highlands of Guatemala, several varieties of hallucinogenic mushrooms grow. One was called *xibalhaj okox* or "underworld mushroom"; another was called *kaizalah okox* or "lost judgment mushroom", clearly referring to their intended use. The employment of other hallucingens such as morning glory seeds, peyote, and the poison of a tropical frog were also available to the Maya for divinatory rituals, but they are not securely documented[15].

During the classic period at least, these substances were not always administered orally. Several painted pottery vessels graphically depict the use of an enema apparatus made of a gourd in apparently ritual settings. The direct introduction of alcoholic or hallucinogenic substances into the colon would result in an immediate absorption by the body, thereby hastening the effect.

---

[13] Vogt, chapter 6.
[14] Norton, p. 20. Smoking illustration from Schele & Miller, p. 155.
[15] Sharer, p. 484.

All this sounds like an elite class on a drug binge and it is more than likely that on occasion personal pleasure trumped ritual divination. However, achieving an altered state of consciousness was a core duty of the shamans, priests, and kings to predict the future.

Blood

Besides interpreting external phenomena like stars and beans, or consuming intoxicants, the Maya engaged in blood letting to communicate with the gods and peer into the future. "Blood was the mortar of ancient Maya life"said Michael Coe in the preface of The Blood Of Kings.[16] Blood was a valuable commodity. According to the Maya view, the gods created humans to sustain and nourish them through the sacrificial offering of blood. In return, the gods brought rain and life-sustaining harvests. Animals such as jaguars were ritually sacrificed on occasion, but most often human captives were the source of divine nutrition.

The victim – man, woman, or child – was stripped, painted blue, and crowned with a peaked headdress. The victim was then led to an altar that was also smeared with blue coloring and bent over it backwards with a costumed assistant holding each arm and leg. Bishop Diego de Landa, who ordered Mayan books burnt, wrote in 1566 of his observation of what happened next: "At this time came the executioner, the nacom, with a knife of stone, and with much skill and cruelty struck him [the sacrificial victim] with the knife between the ribs of his left side under the nipple, and at once plunged his hand in there and seized the heart like a raging tiger, tearing it out alive, and having placed it on a plate, he gave it to the priest, who went

---

[16] Schele and Miller, preface.

quickly and anointed the face of the idols with that fresh blood."[17] Sometimes the body would be thrown down the steps of the temple and skinned and the priest would wear it while dancing with the spectators.

For divination, however, only the ruler's blood and that of his wife would do. Carvings of rulers show them with the sacrificial implements – an obsidian knife and a pouch full of sting ray spines. The male would extend his penis and slice or pierce it to allow a massive flow of blood.   The female would pierce her tongue and draw a thorn-studded cord through it. The blood was collected in a bowl full of paper scraps which would then be burnt. The gods liked their offerings in smoke form.

These blood lettings were often preceded by fasting and accompanied by elaborate ritual and the burning of great quantities of copal incense.   The combination of deprivation, ritual, smoke, pain, and blood loss produced a shock effect that transported the blood letter into a trance state[18]. The direct correlation between blood letting and seeing a vision is graphically depicted in Mayan art. The smoke from the burning blood-soaked papers was imaged as a vision serpent, out of whose mouth a god or ancestor would appear to give advice. It was not for nothing that the rulers of Maya cities were called "blood lords". It was their duty, particularly on important occasions like katuns, to offer their blood to the gods for their people.

It is as instructive to note the methods the Maya apparently did not use – such as examining entrails, dice, meditation, and exhaustive dancing – as it is to note the methods for which they did leave evidence[19]. By whatever means, they

---

[17] Landa, p. 71.
[18] Schele & Miller, p.177.

sought connection to the gods for answers to the mysteries that surrounded them. Their objectives were not unlike peoples in many other cultures, transcending the ordinary dimension of the senses and the mind, to reach other dimensions of reality.

---

[19] Scrying in mirrors or pools of water was sometimes used for divination but this author has not seen images among the Maya that portray it. Miller, p. 80.

Here Lady Balam Ix draws a cord through her tongue and the blood runs down into the bowl full of papers. King Bird Jaguar of Yaxchitlan sits across from her with an awl in his hand preparing to pierce his penis to draw his blood.

Bibliography

Landa, Diego de: Yucatan Before And After The Conquest. Originally written 1566, reprinted by San Fernando undated.

Milbrath, Susan: Star Gods Of The Maya. University of Texas at Austin 1999.

Miller, Mary & Taube, Karl: The Gods And Symbols Of Ancient Mexico And The Maya. Thames & Hudson 1993.

Norton, Marcy: Sacred Gifts, Profane Pleasures. Cornell 2008.

Sharer, Robert: The Ancient Maya 4th edition. Stanford University 1983.

Schele, Linda & Mary Ellen Miller: The Blood Of Kings. Braziller and Kimbell Art Museum 1986.

Schele, Linda; Freidel, David; Parker, Joy: Maya Cosmos. Perennial 1993.

Stuart, David: The Order Of Days. Harmony 2011.

Vogt, Evon: The Zinacantecos Of Mexico. Holt, Rinehardt & Winston 1970.

A NEW TRANSLATION FOR OX WITIK

This paper was first presented at a seminar at Copan in 2010 as part of a lecture series with the Institute for Maya Studies.

The White House

Imagine if you will that the United States as a country has completely vanished and that the entire land mass north of the Rio Grande has reverted back to forest and grassland. Imagine that it is the year 3207 and that Maya archeologists have come north to explore our ancient civilization. Suppose they find an inscription on a pedestal in a ruined city that they think may have been Boston. The inscription is in characters totally foreign to them but after many years of work, they have figured out that the people who built this city used characters to represent sounds alone and not syllables. The partial inscription they found appears to say "John F. Kennedy served in the White House, 1961-1963."

The archeologists figured out a decade ago how this civilization used to mark time and so they can understand the dates. Of course, they don't know if 1961-1963 refers to the time this monument was erected or to some event in the past or in the future. They can also figure out pretty quickly that John F. Kennedy must be a name. Who was he? What position did he hold? Is he one of their gods, a fictional person from their mythology, or a historical figure? Why was he important enough to have this monument erected to him in this place? Those would be puzzling questions, but not as difficult as the next problem.

What is meant by "served" in this context? In the old American language, the verb "to serve" meant to work for, to place food in front of, to be a servant. Yet that doesn't sound important enough to be named on a monument. And what is meant by a "white house?" White is *sak* in the Mayan language and house is *na*. So this John F. Kennedy person is associated in some serving capacity at a *sakna*. What can that possibly mean? Were there other houses colored white and what makes such a house any different from a house colored red, or green, or another color?

Of course, the people who put up the statue understood that "White House" can refer to the presidential residence itself, to the whole body of people who make up a presidential administration, to the executive branch of the American government, or to the president's press secretary. Sometimes even the old Americans were confused and used the term indiscriminately. American democracy, at least as it was originally conceived, saw office holders as public servants. That meaning was much obliterated in the beginning of the 21st Century, but at one time a president was a servant of the people. Who knows what meanings those old Americans attributed to the terms as they were used on this monument? To the 31st Century Maya archeologists exploring the ruins of Boston, this is all a collection of unknown symbols, allegories, metaphors and mysteries.

The same sort of puzzle faces American archeologists as we dig into the Maya past of 1200 years before our own time. Jungle entombed the ancient cities of the Maya homeland and only in the late 19th Century were any serious attempts begun to investigate them. The Mayan inscriptions on temple walls and stelae, as well as writings on pottery, use many symbols, allegories, and metaphors which made perfectly good sense to the people who wrote them but are completely mysterious to us. One example is the verb *ock bi* which translates "to enter the road". What road? The Maya had broad straight roads but why would the action of entering one be significant enough to be memorialized in stone? After much study, we have generally come to understand that *ock bi* is a verb meaning to die or to enter upon the road of death. We have come to understand that the Maya considered death as a journey into Xibalba, the Underworld, and so "entering the road" makes sense. Depending on context, however, it might also mean to enter a tomb to administer post burial rites or to enter a crypt to deposit offerings[20]. Linda Schele in Maya Cosmos discovered that this "road" is also the trunk of the tree of life and furthermore she even equates it to the Milky Way![21] So it is not enough to figure out the literal translation or even the pronunciation for ancient inscriptions. Figuring out the allegories and metaphors is equally important.

So it is with the concept of *ox witik*. *Ox* is the numeral three. *Wi* is the word for "root". *Ti* is a multipurpose preposition that can mean "in", "on", "to", "with", "from" or "at". *Ki* is a phonetic sign but can also mean "heart". So translating strictly from its components, *ox witik* might mean something like "three root from the heart", which makes no sense. However, the components may not be significant at all and the combination of phonetic signs or syllables might produce a word or idea that has an entirely different meaning. In his dictionary of Maya hieroglyphs, John Montgomery shows *witiki* used as an adjective before the noun *ahau* which means "lord". He says this translates into "witik lord" as some kind of title, but he offers no

---

[20] Schele, Code Of Kings p. 157.
[21] Schele, Maya Cosmos p. 76.

translation for *witik*.[22] (Note: the final vowel is often dropped, thus resulting in *witik* instead of *witiki*.) A similar dictionary by Peter Mathews and Peter Biro guesses that *witik* might be a plant name. This is a very questionable hypothesis which even they recognize with a question mark next to their entry.[23] Barbara MacLeod suggested that *tiki* functions here as an aggregate pluralizer, rendering the translation of *ox witik* as "three roots."[24]

The term *ox witik* is found in two inscriptions at Copan in Honduras. The first is on the back of stela B, erected by Eighteen Rabbit on August 20, 731 CE. The second is on top of the famous Altar Q, which was activated by Yax Pac on March 1, 776. The term *witik* without the prefix "three" appears in several other places in Copan. Altar Y has *chul witik ahau* as a title for "holy witik lord". Altar A records *chul witik* without the *ahau* as a place name. Stela 48 has *witik* by itself as a place. On Altar G1, Yax Pac had *chan witik* inscribed which means "four witik." Why he changed from three to four – if indeed he is even referring to the same thing – is yet a mystery.

---

[22] Montgomery, p. 270.
[23] Mathews, The Maya Hieroglyph Dictionary. FAMSI website, www.famsi.org. 2006.
[24] Copan Note #66.

Altar Q

Altar Q contains an important clue to the meaning of *ox witik*. Altar Q is probably the most important dynastic history artifact anywhere in the Maya world. Around its sides are profiles of the sixteen kings of Copan from 427 to 776 CE. Each sits upon his own name glyph or euphemism that refers to him. Yax Kuk Mo, the founder of the dynasty, sits upon an *ahau* glyph, meaning "lord". All the kings are lords, of course, but the fact that this lord is sitting on that particular glyph most likely indicates that he was considered by the Copan elite as the supreme lord. The elements of his headdress spell out his full name.

The top of the altar tells the story of his coming to Copan and establishing the dynasty and ends with a reference to

Yax Pac, the king who commissioned the altar. In this way the latter, who is the 16th to rule at Copan, is attempting to show his legitimate right to govern through direct descent from the 1st ruler. (Illustration of the top of Altar Q from Copan Note 66.)

The translation of the inscription on top of Altar Q begins: "On September 5, 426, lord Kuk Mo received the Kawil scepter at the Root Tree House [crossed bundles with peek-a-boo head]." David Stuart holds that there is no clear phonetic value yet assigned for the crossed bundles glyph[25], although John Montgomery in his dictionary indicates *ch'ok* as a possibility[26]. The "root tree house" is clearly indicated by the *wi-te-naah* glyphs below and behind the crossed bundles. The crossed bundles *wi-te-naah* place is used in exactly the same context in other Maya cities[27]. Fash and Tokovinine have identified the crossed bundles with the House of New Fire at Teotihuacan[28] where new kings received their authority to rule. Yax Kuk Mo traveled to Teotihuacan for just that purpose[29]

The important point for our purpose here is that the *wi* glyph very definitely means "root" as in "origins" rather than as a botanical term. So if *wi* has any bearing in and of itself on the definition of *witik*, it is as an origin or source. Therefore the term *ox witik* at least contains a sense of a "three source" place or thing.

---

[25] Bell, p. 236.

[26] Montgomery, p. 269.

[27] For example, Quirigua zoomorph P and Rio Amarillo structure 5. Tikal stela 31 has a *wi-ti-naah* glyph in its early form, without the crossed bundles, at F5 and again at E15.

[28] Fash, see bibliography.

[29] Van Cleve, see bibliography.

Altar Q goes on to say: "On February 8, 727, the Lord of the West (Yax Kuk Mo) came to the end of his journey. There are a number of uncertainties in this section of the text, specifically at D2 and D4. Schele speculated that glyph C5 suffixed with *li-ha* may mean to establish or draw boundaries.[30] This could refer to the layout of the great plaza of Copan – and strata samples there indicate that at least part of the plaza was laid out in Yax Kuk Mo's time – however the meaning remains unclear. Glyph D5 is *ox witik*. Schele suggested several times in her lectures and writings that *ox witik* may refer to the acropolis at Copan or some feature of it. It is my hypothesis that Eighteen Rabbit on stela B tells us exactly what *ox witik* really is.

Stela B

Eighteen Rabbit raised up stela B on the major katun ending date of 9.15.0.0.0 when he was 50 years old and 36 years into his reign[31]. Stela B is a remarkable political statement in stone. On its face, Eighteen Rabbit is shown in a standard pose decked out in the full panoply of royal regalia. At his belt are pouches of sting ray spines for his blood letting while from his body grow tendrils of maize – symbolizing the central role of his blood sacrifice to renew the fertility of the earth and therefore his central role in the cycle of life for his people. Elizabeth Newsome, in her exhaustive work Trees Of Paradise And Pillars Of The World, describes in detail the artistic and symbolic elements of this amazing monument, but for our purposes I wish to call attention its major theme.

---

[30] Copan Note #66.
[31] Van Cleve, bibliography.

Stela B shows Eighteen Rabbit stepping out of a mountain. At his feet are the lower jaws of the mountain monster and over his head are the upper jaws. Up the sides are mountain masks to emphasize the point. Newsome makes a very good case for the similarity of this iconography to the façade of Temple 22 which Eighteen Rabbit completed sixteen years earlier[32]. That building's outer entrance is caught in the jaws of a mountain monster very much like stela B and it has masks up all four corners. Temple 22 was Eighteen Rabbit's personal temple to replace Rosalila which he carefully buried. Rosalila is the name archeologists give to the shrine built over the tomb of the founder, Yax Kuk Mo. *(photo by author)*

The mountain monster's upper jaws on stela B are overlaid by huge macaw beaks that early explorers took for elephant trunks. The eyes of the mountain monster are not ordinary mountain monster eyes but rather those of a quetzal macaw. This, then, is no ordinary mountain from which Eighteen Rabbit steps forth. It is in  fact the *mo witz*, the "macaw mountain." In fact, the inscription on the south side boldly states that stela B was

---

[32] Newsome, p. 137.

erected *ubah mo witz ahau*, "in the image of the Macaw Mountain lord."[33]   Others have speculated where this macaw mountain could be, but the mountains around the Copan valley are quite undistinguished and there are no artifacts or remains that indicate that the people of the region considered any one of them to be at all special. The only other candidate for a macaw mountain is a mountain constructed by human hands, specifically the pyramid mountain constructed over the tomb of First Quetzal Macaw himself – Yax Kuk Mo, the venerated founder of the dynasty. This pyramid is designated by archeologists as 10L-16, directly in over Rosalila and in front of which Yax Pac centered his Altar Q.

---

[33] Newsome, p. 181.

North   South

The patron of Yax
counted the year   It was planted
                                        in the ground

                                        Great Sky God
9 baktuns   Chak was its name

                                        It was in the image
15 katuns   of Macaw Mountain

0 tuns   Lord

0 unials   Thus has been
                                        completed

0 kins   300 years

4 Ahau   he scattered
                                        his offering

13 Yax   and conjured
                                        the image of the

when the heart
was empty   Fiery God

of the God of
Heaven and   Kawill, God of
                                        lineages
when the heart
was empty
                                        the 13th successor
                                        of the founder
of the God of Earth

when the heart   Eighteen Rabbit
was empty of
One Sky-in-Hand,
                                        holy blood lord
lord of the 16   of Copan
Yookins?

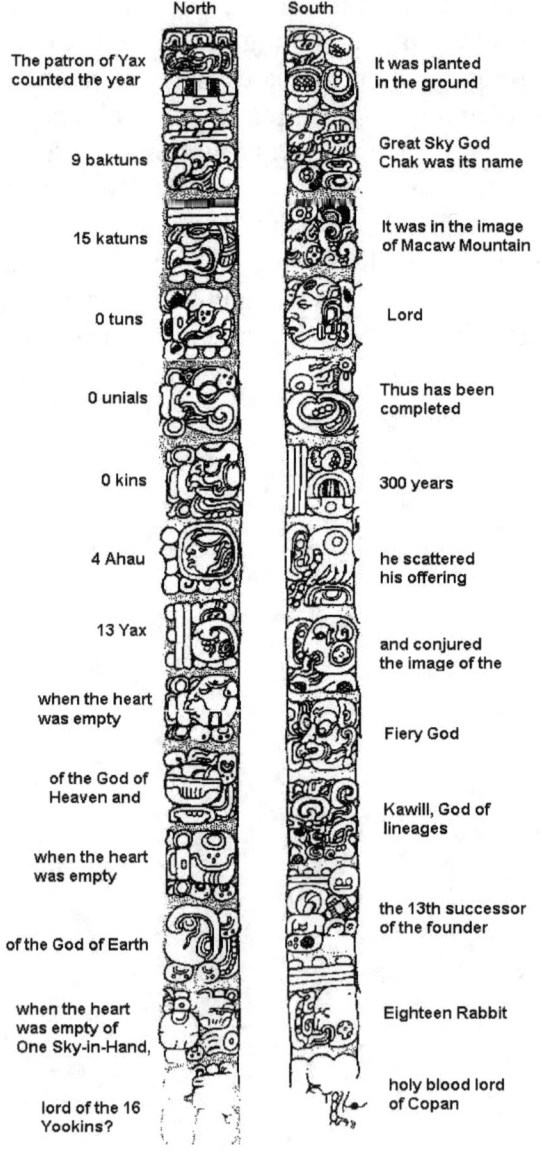

44

The illustration to the right is from the <u>Code of Kings</u>[34]. It declares that stela B was commissioned on 9.15.0.0.0 or August 16, 731, when three named Gods' hearts were empty. The south side declares the formal name of the stela and stipulates that it is in the image of the Macaw Mountain Lord.

The next phrase is key: "Thus was completed 15 katuns" or 300 years which harks back to 431 during the reign of Yax Kuk Mo. Eighteen Rabbit goes on to say that he is the 13th successor to the founder. These two statements add weight to the *mo witz* iconography to link this stela to the tomb of Yax Kuk Mo.

There are more clues on the back of the stela which itself is entirely given over to a huge representation of the mountain monster. In the monster's headdress is an ancestor figure with an oversized hat that calls to mind the tasseled head pieces worn by the Teotihuacan invaders who conquered Tikal in 378 CE. Newsome suggests that the ancestor figure on the back of stela B is the supreme lord and dynastic founder, Yax Kuk Mo.[35] In fact, Yax Kuk Mo hailed from the Tikal area, was a child or a young man at the time of the invasion, and was a soldier of Tikal when he came to take over Copan. Given the rest of the iconography on this monument, it is entirely reasonable to conclude that this ancestor representation is indeed the founder.

---

[34] Schele, <u>Code Of Kings</u>, p. 164.
[35] Newsome, p. 141.

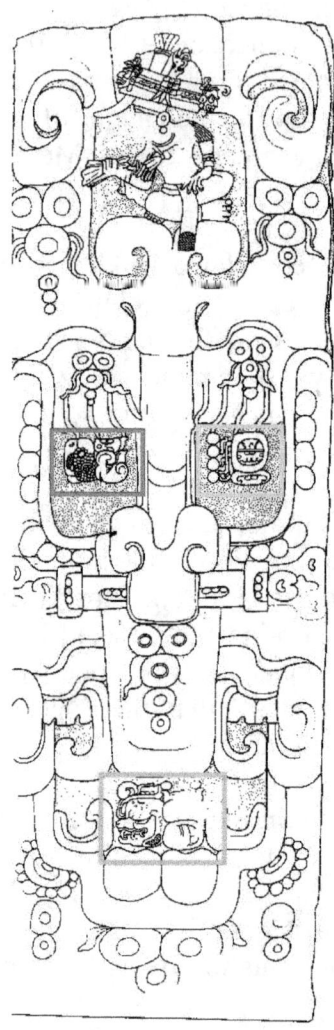

There are also three glyphs on the back of the stela – one in each eye of the monster and one in its mouth. The first glyph is *mo witz*, which again refers to "macaw mountain." The second glyph is *kan na kan*, or "four houses of the sky" which refers to a centering of the four prime directions. At Copan, the "four skies" is a frequent term (it is used several times on stela A). It is a grounding and centering term which here is best translated as "ground zero". The final glyph is *baknal ox witik*, which means "bone place three source." To interpret what that glyph means, we have to look up into the sky[36].

---

[36] Agurcia, p. 133 for some reason neglects to account for the last two glyphs.

Turtle and Hearthstones

The Maya were keen astronomers and developed their own interpretations of the night sky. They noted the band of the Milky Way and the ellipse of the planets. They identified constellations and assigned various animals to them and developed their own zodiac which operates similarly to our western one. In fact, Scorpio is the same in both. Susan Milbrath has written a brilliant study of Maya astronomy, Star Gods Of The Maya, in which she examines the connections between astronomical observations and Mayan iconography and inscriptions. In particular, she points to the three bright stars in Orion's belt – Alnitak, Alnilam, and Mintaka. These are the Maya constellation of the turtle. They are clearly portrayed as such in the cartouches from the north wall of room 2 at Bonampak and in the Madrid Codex.

The turtle is very important in Maya iconography. The turtle is the mountain monster whose shell cracks open to bring forth the maize god. The turtle is the symbol of the cycle of life, death, and rebirth. The Maya marked the beginning of the current age (August 13, 3114 BCE) by the appearance of the turtle constellation in the eastern sky.[37]

The star Alnitak is also part of the constellation of the hearthstones. Alnitak, Saiph, and Rigel in the constellation Orion form a triangle just below and part of the turtle. The Maya called them *ox ibxkub*, the "three hearth stars" and Nebula 42 in the center of them is *kak*, or "fire." The relation of the hearthstones to the turtle is very graphically illustrated in the Madrid Codex, where the turtle carries the three hearthstone stars in tripod formation on its back.[38]

---

[37] Schele, Maya Cosmos. p. 66
[38] Milbrath, p. 252.

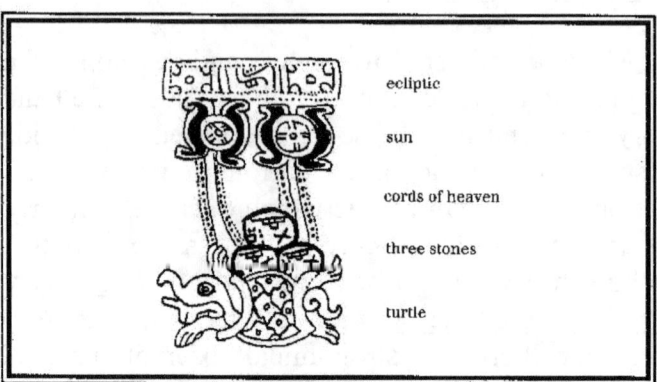

ecliptic

sun

cords of heaven

three stones

turtle

FIGURE 2:16 Detail from the Madrid Codex

The hearthstones are the center of the Maya universe. Matthew Looper, in Lightning Warrior, translates the creation myth from Quirigua stela C[39]: "At the beginning of the current age (August 13, 3114 BCE) the tripod is manifested. Three stones are bundled. Jaguar Paddler and Stingray Paddler plant a stone; it was at First Five Sky?; it was a jaguar throne stone. Ik Nah Chak? plants a stone; it happened at large town?; it was a snake throne stone. Itzamna bundled a stone; it was a water throne stone. It happened at Lying Down Sky, the First Three Stone Place, that the thirteen baktuns were completed. This happened under the supervision of the *wak chan ahau*." Schele determined that the *wak chan* is really *wakah chan* – the Milky Way.[40] (She also demonstrates that the Lying Down Sky is the Milky Way at nightfal when it appears to rest on the horizon. Later in the night its angle tilts vertical and becomes the Standing Up Sky.) In other words, the

[39] Looper, p.226.

[40] Schele, Maya Cosmos, p. 76. She concluded as well that the Milky Way and the trunk of the World Tree are one and the same.

beginning of the current age happened when the Milky Way, Orion's belt (turtle), and the Hearthstones were in a certain celestial position.

Schele reported the connection between the hearth stars of the sky and the hearth stones of the kitchen. "As the hearthstones surround the cooking fire and establish the center of the home, so the three stone thrones of Creation centered the cosmos and allowed the sky to be lifted from the Primordial Sea."[41] Because the stones were laid before the sky was lifted, they were laid on earth as well as in the sky. The connection for the Maya was clear and direct. Dennis Tedlock says that the three stars even today are represented in the three hearthstones of the typical Quiche kitchen fireplace, arranged to form a triangle with the fire in the center.[42] When Yax Pac assembled his three G altars next to Eighteen Rabbit's stelae in Copan's central plaza, he arranged them in a tripod grouping of three. Perhaps he was attempting to "reheat" the Copan dynasty after Eighteen Rabbit's untimely death.

As in the heavens, so also on earth, the three hearthstones represent for the Maya a place of origin, foundation, center, beginning, and source for all that follows. This comes very close to the meaning of *ox witik* as a "three source" place or thing. Could *ox witik* and *ox ibxkub* be referring to the same thing? Could we express their meaning more accurately by translating them the same way as we use the concept of "cornerstone"? The three stars in Orion are the cornerstone of creation. The three stones of a Mayan kitchen are the cornerstone of the home and family. Could *ox witik* be another way of using the concept of

---

[41] Schele, Maya Cosmos, p. 67.
[42] Schele, Maya Cosmos, p. 79.

hearthstones as a cornerstone of something that was fundamental to the kings of Copan?

The Bone Place

The cornerstone of the dynasty at Copan and the royal power it exercised was Yax Kuk Mo. Back on Altar Q, the text of C5 and D5 reads: *jul-li-ja ox witik*, which translates "he arrived or he drew the boundaries, *ox witik*. *Ox witik* has been interpreted as a place, as in a place where he arrived. But in Mayan, the subject follows the object which follows the verb. Therefore, it may be that *ox witik* is the subject of the verb to arrive; it could be the one arriving instead of the place arrived at. Perhaps *ox witik* is a metaphor for the beginning of the dynasty, Yax Kuk Mo, just as "five katun lord" is a metaphor for the 12th ruler, Smoke Jaguar. So *jul-li-ja ox witik* could be translated as "the *ox witik* arrived".

We use the word "cornerstone" for both places and people. We speak of the US Constitution as the cornerstone of our nation, even though it is paper and not stone. The christian bible speaks of "the stone the builders rejected has become the cornerstone" – an allegory for the rejection of the prophet Jesus by the Jewish authorities. Yax Kuk Mo was the cornerstone of the Copan royal dynasty and his tomb was the tangible cornerstone of their political and spiritual life.

Eighteen Rabbit makes this abundantly clear on stela B with the three glyphs on the back. The mountain monster out of which he emerges is the *mo witz*, the "macaw mountain". It is the *kan na kan*, the "four houses of the sky", the center of the universe, ground zero. Most tellingly, it is the *baknal ox witik*, the "bone place cornerstone." Bone rituals among the Maya were common.

Altar 5 at Tikal illustrates one in progress. William Fash, et al. describe their findings in the Motmot Tomb at Copan wherein the bones of a young adult female were revisited after burial, rearranged, and burnt.[43] The tombs of Yax Kuk Mo and the female in the Margarita Tomb believed to be his wife were re-entered several times and both skeletons were covered in cinnabar after the flesh had decayed. Eighteen Rabbit himself states quite directly that he oversaw a ritual in which his grandfather Butz Chan's bones were cut. He recorded the act on stela A, dedicated on February 1, 731, just seven months before the events outlined on stela B.

The only bone place that is the cornerstone of Copan, the center of its universe, and associated with a Macaw Mountain is the tomb of Yax Kuk Mo. It is located under structure 10L-16, not Temple 22. Eighteen Rabbit is therefore declaring to all who look

Baknal *Ox Witik*
Bone Place Three Sources

From the back of
Copan stela B

upon stela B that he literally went into the tomb of the founder and there performed a ritual. Stela B is a representation of him emerging from the Macaw Mountain tomb of the founder after he was finished. *Ox witik* therefore is either the remains of the founder, his final resting place as the cornerstone king, or the revered temple which housed his remains. It would have been quite clear to the Maya which meaning to ascribe to the term *ox witik* from the context, just as we today know which meaning to ascribe to the term "The White House."

---

[43] Bell, p. 68.

Bibliography

FAMSI is the Foundation for the Advancement of Mesoamerican Studies, Inc.

Agurcia Fasquelle, Ricardo, ed.:   Manual De Los Monumentos De Copan, Honduras. vol 1. Asociacion Copan 2010.

Bell, Ellen; Canuto, Marcello; Sharer, Robert, eds.: Understanding Early Classic Copan.   University of Pennsylvania Museum of Archeology and Anthropology 2004.

Copan Note #66. "A Brief Commentary on the Top of Altar Q" – 1989. Linda Schele.

Fash, Barbara & William and Tokovinine, Alexandre: The House Of New Fire At Teotihuacan And Its Legacy In Mesoamerica. Harvard 2009. http://isites.harvard.edu/fs/docs/icb.topic1173827.files/Fash _New20%Fire_2009.pdf.

Looper, Matthew: Lightning Warrior. University of Texas at Austin 2003.

Mathews, Peter & Biro, Peter: The Maya Hieroglyph Dictionary. FAMSI website, www.famsi.org. 2006.

Milbrath, Susan: Star Gods Of The Maya. University of Texas at Austin 1999.

Montgomery, John: Dictionary Of Maya Hieroglyphs. Hippocrene 2002.

Newsome, Elizabeth: Trees Of Paradise And Pillars Of The World. University of Texas at Austin 2001.

Schele, Linda & Matthews, Peter: Code Of Kings. Scribner 1998.

Schele, Linda, Freidel, David & Parker, Joy: Maya Cosmos. Harper Collins 1995.

Schele, Linda; Freidel, David; Parker, Joy: Maya Cosmos. Harper Collins 1995.

Van Cleve, Janice: Yax Kuk Mo – Mover And Shaker In The Maya World. CreateSpace 2010.

A TALE OF TWO CITIES

The Valley

Anyone who has walked the one mile path from the little village of Copan Ruinas in the western hills of Honduras to the archeological park of Copan cannot help but be struck by the beauty of this valley. The hills are green with pine trees and coffee plants. The lowlands are ripe with chilies, vegetables, and corn. Cowboys round up their stray bovines along the highway while police at the checkpoint doze in the shade of their patio.

Then you see it – a giant monolith perched on a platform beside the road. This is stela 5, with the stern image of the 11th king of Copan, Butz Chan, glaring down from one side and his grim son and successor, Smoke Jaguar, standing on the other side. Between them a single column of glyphs runs down the left and right sides while before each of them rest large round "drum" altars with glyphs around their edges. Under this imposing statement in stone is a tomb, open now and empty, its contents in the village museum. A short distance away in a horse pasture stands stela 6. This one also shows Smoke Jaguar and the inscription announces the arrival of his son, Eighteen Rabbit. Stela 6 is somewhat smaller than stela 5 and like the other it is sheltered from the weather by a tin roof.

What are these monuments doing way out here, a half mile from the archeological park with its storied Acropolis? The answer is: they are not "way out here". In fact, this entire valley is dotted with the remains of monuments and buildings left from the brilliant kingdom of Copan which dominated the entire region of western Honduras and eastern Guatemala even up into what is now Belize between 400 and 800 CE. A map displaying some of the structures so far surveyed is available at www.mesoweb.com/copan/resources/media/cop07003308.jpg.

A large number of major compounds – complete with palaces, courtyards, and outbuildings – have been discovered in all directions outside the main Acropolis and grand plaza at the center of Copan. The largest ones line the *sacbe* or highway that extends east and west of the grand plaza. Along the eastern section are the "gated communities" of the rich and famous called today Las Sepulturas in Spanish for all the tombs that have been discovered there. Beneath these structures lies evidence of some of the earliest occupation of this valley.

At the west end of the *sacbe* rose a huge complex which archeologists have dubbed "Comendero". An excellent interactive map with explanations, photos, and even a digital reconstruction may be found at www.papacweb.org/copan.html. This complex is just a few yards beyond stelae 5 and 6. Southwest of the Acropolis is another densely built up area called "El Bosque" because it is deeply forested. Here are many mounds as yet unexplored, a charming small ballcourt (perhaps for the Maya Little Leagues), and Tomb 1 – not to be confused with Tomb 1 just south of the acropolis where the famous Copan engraved peccary skull was found. Today a beautiful nature walk with well done informative signs courses through El Bosque, inviting the visitor to a less crowded appreciation of the Maya world.

The Village

One of the most important sites in the Copan valley has unfortunately not benefited from the protective embrace of the forest. The high ground west of the archeological park which today is the village of Copan Ruinas was, in ancient times, a major settlement in itself. There archeologists such as Alfred Maudsley (1850-1931) and Sylvanus Morley (1883-1948) toiled for many years uncovering fragments of monuments which had been broken up by villagers to use in walls, foundations, and road pavements. Morley writes about stela 9:

"It was intact in 1910, when the writer first visited Copan, but when Spinden was there two years later he found that, together with stela 8, it had been broken up to form the foundation of an adobe wall then in course of construction around the cemetery. This unpardonable act of vandalism, although greatly to be lamented, is not irreparable, since excellent casts exist of both destroyed monuments."[44]

During his work at Copan, Maudsley made plaster and paper mache casts of all the monuments he could find in addition to taking excellent photographs and notes. In many cases his casts and photographs are all that remains of once existing inscriptions. How many more were destroyed is impossible to tell. Such loss is not unique to Copan, of course, as the remains of the ancient Mediterranean civilizations often found themselves poached for Christian churches.

The timely investigations by these and other archeologists have fortunately recovered a good many monuments and fragments from the village area. These have found their

---

[44] Morley, p. 93.

way into the local museum whose small size is incommensurate with the treasures it contains. The early archeologists were even able to map out certain structures still existing at the time and to discover the original locations of some of the altars and stelae. Morley includes a detailed and annotated map of the village as it was when he was there and he locates the finds in his book, The Inscriptions At Copan[45].

Morley's map includes the location of fragments, places to which items had been removed, and names of the then current owners of the properties where the items were found. The author has redrawn the map below to highlight only those structures and monuments whose dates and original locations were verified by the archeologists. Fragments and secondary locations are dimmed as are the current street patterns. This gives, hopefully, a better sense of the "second" city of Copan prior to the attritions of the villagers.

---

[45] Morley, p. 124.

MONUMENTS FOUND IN COPAN RUINAS (GROUP 9)
from Morley "The Inscriptions At Copan" p. 124

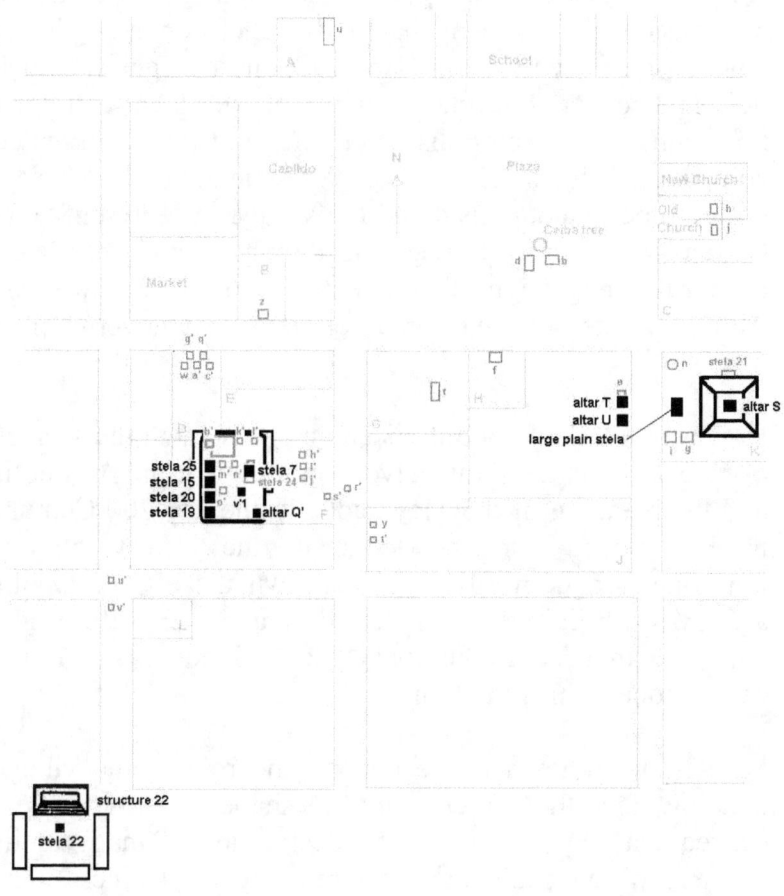

The Second City

It might be a stretch to consider these remains as evidence of a "second" city of Copan. Linda Schele, an archeologist whose prolific writings and translations brought so much light and color to our understanding of the Maya world, did not think the Acropolis and the village represented competing polities, but instead were one entity.[46] Morley, on the other hand, considered the village to represent "Old Copan" where city life began in the valley and only later, during the long reign of Smoke Jaguar (628-695), was the Acropolis site selected for a religious and governmental center.[47]

However, Morley had only been able to scratch the surface of Copan in his day. Intensive exploration at the Acropolis and the breaking of the Maya code in the late 20th Century have exploded our knowledge of the history of this important kingdom. It is now known that the Acropolis area was a religious and political center even before Yax Kuk Mo invaded in February 427 CE and made it the cornerstone of his kingdom.[48]

What is not known is the history and role of the village area, owing to the obliteration of its shape and structures by subsequent occupation and the destruction of many of its features which could have offered important clues. The best we have are the findings of the early archeologists who

---

[46] Schele, Copan Note #70, p. 8

[47] Morley, p.210, pp. 415-431.

[48] See Bell et al: Understanding Early Classic Copan, Braswell: The Maya And Teotihuacan, and Van Cleve: The Founder, among many current resources.

happened upon the scene almost too late to record what was left.

The map shows in bold the features in the village of whose original location Morley was confident. Dimmed on the map are the locations where these items and other fragments were found but which were not their original locations. Highlighting in this manner reveals three main areas in the village where significant remains of "Old Copan" were uncovered. For reference, stelae 5 and 6 are located just east off the map and stelae 8 and 9 were located just west. A consideration of each of the three main areas in the village is in order.

Structure 22. Archeologists found a fragment of a stela in the courtyard of structure 22. The structure is typical of a small clan compound with living quarters surrounding a courtyard. It is unusual to find a stela in Copan in such a place and Morley suggested that perhaps it could have been an altar. At the Maya compound in Teotihuacan called Tetitla, there is such a clan altar located in its the courtyard. This fragment, called stela 22, includes five damaged glyphs on one side. No date can be read from this, yet Morley determined that the style is archaic, belonging to the period 495-534 CE[49]. If structure 22 was a domestic compound, it must have been highly honored and unusual to have its own stela. If, on the other hand, the building it fronted had a religious significance, then a stela before it would perhaps be more plausible.

---

[49] Morley, p. 68.

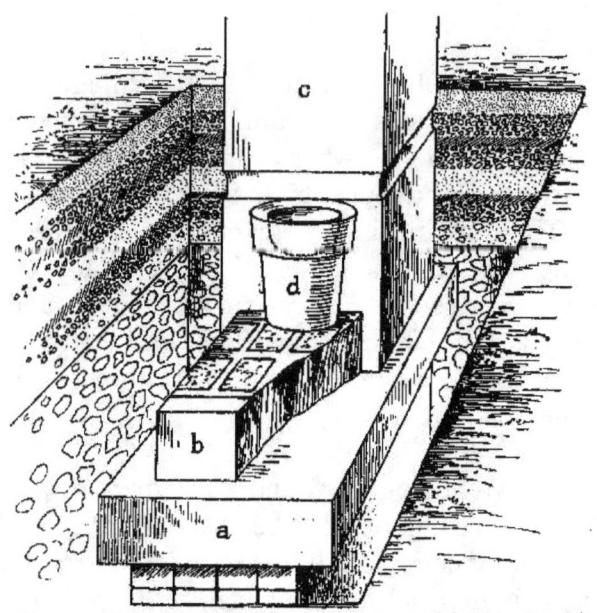

FIG. 12.—Sketch showing position of fragment of Stela 24 found in 1916, resting on foundation-stone of Stela 7: *a*, foundation-stone of Stela 7; *b*, fragment of Stela 24; *c*, Stela 7; *d*, small altar with depression in top.

Central Mound. Near the center of the village was a mound, approximately 88 ft long from north to south, 56 ft wide east to west, rising almost 3 feet from the surface of the ground.[50] On this mound, Morley found what he determined were the original locations for five stelae and an altar. Many fragments were also determined to have come from this mound. Stela 7 had fallen and broken in two right next to its foundation vault and therefore this is considered its original location. Today it stands in the small courtyard of the village museum. Interred in the foundation is the fragment of stela 24 which was reused as an offering for stela 7. In this illustration by Morley, stela 24 is shown at *b* under the "bucket" altar.

[50] Morley, p. 103.

Four other stelae – 25, 15, 20, and 18 – line the back of the mound according to the map. This is unusual placement for Copan – lined up in a row along the edge of a mound. Most stelae at Copan stand alone with their altar before them and even Eighteen Rabbit's cluster in the grand plaza are spaced apart. The mound itself is unusual, resembling neither a platform nor a temple. That the Maya moved some or all four of these stelae to this location cannot be ruled out, considering they moved or reused so many other monuments.

East Pyramid. Near the east edge of the village was a pyramid topped by an altar. In front of it rested a large plain stela and two more altars. The large plain stela cannot be dated. Altars S, T, and U have been dated to kings late in the dynastic history of Copan. When this pyramid was being dismantled in 1916, a fragment of stela 21 was discovered buried in its core. All that is left of this piece is the introductory glyphs at the top so its original provenance and dedication date remain unknown.

Dating The Monuments

The row of stelae on the mound in the center of the village were thought by Morley to be the oldest in the valley, which he used to support his hypothesis that Copan's religious and governmental center began at the village and only later moved the Acropolis. Now, however, with the discovery of the Xukpi stone, the Motmot Marker, Stela 63 and the tombs of Yax Kuk Mo and his queen, it is known that the dynasty was founded at the Acropolis and the center of government and religion remained there.

However, the dates on the monuments in the village do reveal that the kings did not ignore the village area and indeed continued to raise monuments there throughout the dynasty's 400 year history. A table of the village monuments with their dates and the reigns of the dynastic rulers are displayed below:

Monument	Date	Ruler and dates of reign
Stela 18	Aug 26, 455	Popol Hol (432-470)
Stela 20	Jul 4, 465	
Stela 24	Mar 21, 485	Cu Ix (477-494) later deposited under
stela 7 by Butz Chan		
Stela 25[51]	Mar 21, 485	
Altar Q'	Aug 24, 524	Waterlily Jaguar
(504-544)		
Stela 15	Aug 24, 524	
Altar X[52]	Dec 8, 553	Moon Jaguar (553-
578)		
		later deposited under
stela 5 by Smoke Jaguar		
Stela 9	Jan 27, 564	
Stela 22	??	later deposited under
the pyramid of altar S		

---

[51] Schele, in Copan Note #70, proposes that stelae 25 could be a broken piece of stela 24.

[52] Agurcia attributes this altar to Sak Lu, the 9th king of Copan, (551-553).

Stela 7	May 10, 613	Butz Chan (578-628)
Stela 5	Feb 6, 628[53]	Smoke Jaguar (628-695)
Stela 5e	Sep 16, 657	
Stela 5w	Jul 17, 667	
Stela 6	May 8, 682	
Altar S	Aug 20, 731	Eighteen Rabbit (695-738)
Altar U	Jun 30, 763	Yax Pac (763-821)
Altar T	Mar 17, 783	
Stela 8	Mar 22, 783	

---

[53] Morley's dates for stela 5 and its two altars are contravened in Copan Note 31 by Schele and Stuart.

A Fragmented Monarchy

On April 25, 738, the 13th king of Copan, Eighteen Rabbit, was captured in battle, tortured, and killed six days later by his cousin[54], Cauac Sky. The latter was the ruler of nearby Quirigua which until that moment had been subordinate to Copan. This event changed everything. Copan's political and religious prestige was shattered and its economy was shaken. Smoke Monkey succeeded Eighteen Rabbit 39 days later, but the monopoly on power once tightly controlled by the kings, now had to be shared with the leading nobles. Smoke Monkey rebuilt the Chachalaka structure on the Acropolis to reflect the new reality. Mat patterns, symbols of authority, were woven in stone over the doorways and around the upper register were carved the coats of arms of the nine leading clan chiefs. It was now the Popol Nah or council house where governance was shared with the upper nobility.

This state of affairs continued through the rule of the next king, Smoke Shell. No monuments have been found in the village securely identified with either of these two rulers[55]. Their attention was focused on the famous Hieroglyphic

---

[54] Cauac Sky was the brother of Smoke Monkey, both cousins of Eighteen Rabbit. Copan Note 98 and Van Cleve, Eighteen Rabbit.

[55] Altars B' and C' were originally located at the base of 10L-7 in the courtyard of the Hieroglyphic Stairway and dated by Morley to between 761 and 771. However, Morley's map shows items B' and C' in the village. Altar C' names Butz Chan as holy blood lord of Copan and therefore would seem to date before 628. Altar B' names Yax Kuk Mo and what may be a "twelfth from the founder" glyph which would be Smoke Jaguar. Morley, plate 22.

Stairway and its courtyard at the Acropolis where they tried to rejuvenate the luster of royal kingship.

Things changed on June 30, 763, when the 16th king, Yax Pac, acceded to the throne of Copan. From the start, he appears to have "seated" in almost equal power, his brothers Yahau Chan Ah Bac, Yax Kamlay[56], and Yaku Chac[57]. Yahau Chan Ah Bac was the son of Ix Xok[58], the princess of Palenque who was imported to Copan by Smoke Monkey to marry his son, Smoke Shell, and thus renew the prestige of the royal house. Yax Pac, Yax Kamlay, and Yaku Chac were born of this marriage. When Smoke Shell died, Ix Xok married a prominent nobleman, "Knot" Skull, and Yahau Chan Ah Bac was born of that marriage.[59]

Yax Pac began his reign by continuing to focus on the Acropolis. In his first ten years he constructed the massive temple 11 and its reviewing stand, multiplied the altars before temple 7, and consecrated the first of his three snake altars in the grand plaza. However, he was forced by circumstances and precedent to distribute royal privileges even beyond his brothers. On Dec 7, 774, he dedicated a carved bench for a noble in Las Sepulturas that was a gift to this person by Smoke Shell.[60]

Nor was this an isolated incident. A year and a half later Yax Pac dedicated altar W' in another compound in Las

---

[56] "Yax Kamlay" means "first administrator" and is a title, not a personal name. Copan Note 77.

[57] Copan Note 98.

[58] See Copan Notes 5, 20, and 77. Also Schele: Forest of Kings and Van Cleve: Eighteen Rabbit.

[59] Copan Note 20 and Van Cleve: Eighteen Rabbit.

[60] Schele, Forest of Kings, p. 329.

Sepulturas to the 3rd successor of a clan chief named "Skull". Apparently the first chief of this clan received permission from Eighteen Rabbit to built a lavish compound because he was the king's favorite ball player[61]. The name "Skull" is significant because Ix Xok, Yax Pac's mother, married one "Knot" Skull and produced his half brother, Yahau Chan Ah Bac.[62] It is likely that "Knot" Skull is the third successor of the ball player. The exterior of another building in the "gated community" sports a mat pattern of authority on its front. An undated bench in a major compound[63] at the eastern end of Las Sepulturas may also have been granted by Yax Pac during this time.

Yax Pac did not ignore the village, either. He joined his half brother in a ritual ceremony there on March 17, 783, and allowed him to commission Altar T in his own name. Five days later the king raised stela 8 in the village area, naming his half brother and emphasizing that they both came from the same mother.[64] In June of that year, he dedicated altar G' to his third brother, Yaku Chak[65] which was found by archeologists upside down in the Bosque area. In 793, Yahau Chan Ah Bac dedicated altar U in the village. On it, he celebrates the accession of the king and the "seating" of Yax Kamlay, and names his father "Knot" Skull and mother Ix Xoc and repeats that the latter is also the mother of Yax Pac.[66]

---

[61] This is 9N-82 "House of the Bacabs". Schele, Forest of Kings, p. 491 note 61.

[62] Van Cleve, Who Was Eighteen Rabbit?

[63] This is 8N-66.

[64] Schele, Forest of Kings. p. 330.

[65] Copan Note 89.

[66] Schele, Forest of Kings. p 333 and Copan Notes 3, 5, and 20.

On the same day, September 13, 795, that Yax Pac commissioned altar G2 in the grand plaza, Yahau Chan Ah Bac left a carved stone in the Popol Nah council house. It names himself and Yax Kamlay and celebrates the king's accession. Stela 29, found in the east court of the Acropolis is a twin stone to the one in the Popol Nah. It was dedicated the same day and it, too, names Yax Kamlay. The third brother was not forgotten. He is named on altar F' (dated 798) and another altar (dated 802) found in the king's own compound south of the Acropolis.[67] Yax Pac returned to the Skull clan compound in 813[68] to join Mak Chanil, the current clan chief, to dedicate the carved bench in his residence.

One last item of note is that altar U identifies Yax Pac's father and it is not the previous king, Smoke Shell.[69] The name of this man is not confirmed by existing evidence but the Hieroglyphic Stairway identifies a brother of Smoke Shell named Bolon Yokte Chul who may or may not have sired Yax Pac.

Conclusions

Some form of central power existed in the area of the Copan Acropolis before Yax Kuk Mo arrived and all the kings who succeeded him focused their center there. Nevertheless they continued to raise monuments in the village throughout the history of the dynasty. When Yax Pac died, sometime before 820, the dynasty died with him and his contemporaries knew it. Stela 11 was raised next to his tomb on the Acropolis on May 4, 820. It says that "the

---

[67] Copan Notes 72 and 89.
[68] Copan Note 23.
[69] Copan Note 98

dynasty of the founder came to an end with the death of the Eighteen Images of the War Serpent, Sun-Eyed Yax Pac, the two katun (40 year) ruler."[70]

Without a viable king, the Acropolis fell into disuse. Its grandiose temples and lavish rituals no longer had a monarchy to support. However the clan structure and its noble elite continued. The population dropped by two thirds in the 200 years after Yax Pac's death yet about 14% of them in 1000 CE still lived in the clan compounds[71]. The nobles were still constructing grand houses for themselves and some of these undoubtedly thrived in the Bosque and in Las Sepulturas no less than in the village.

The Bosque and Las Sepulturas were eventually abandoned, but the village was probably never without inhabitants. There were still farmers there in 1576 when Diego Garcia de Palacio visited and asked them about the ruins.[72] Stephens and Catherwood sheltered in the village with farmers while exploring the ruins in Copan in 1839[73].

Yet the village does not stand out at any time as an independent or unusual center of importance that in any way competed with the central core of Copan at the Acropolis. There were stelae erected in the village but there were also stelae erected up an down the Copan valley and in the hills around it. Yahau Chan Ah Bac or Yax Kamlay may have governed from palaces located at the

---

[70] Schele, Forest of Kings, p. 343. She saw Eighteen Rabbit's name in the inscription but it clearly reads *waxaklajun ubah chan*.
[71] Webster, et al. p.167.
[72] Letter of Diego Garcia de Palacio to King Philip II of Spain, in Morley p. 541.
[73] Stephens, p. 109ff.

village but there were other large clan compounds scattered throughout the valley as well. The village never achieved its own emblem glyph like Rio Amarillo or Quirigua, nor did it ever acquire a coat of arms for itself other than what might have been represented by those of any of the other clan chieftains figured on the Popol Nah. Finally, the population studies by Webster et al. do not reveal a density of habitation at the village any larger than the densities of El Bosque or Las Sepulturas[74].

On the other hand, the village is the only place outside the Acropolis that possessed a pyramid with an altar on top (altar S). The strange central mound where so many monuments were erected or repositioned is also unique to the village. The fact that two of the last king's brothers, apparently equal to him in power, apparently held office there and they and the king left monuments there describing their relationships also points to a special status to the village area. It was probably not a separate city but it appears to have been more important than the suburbs of Las Sepulturas or El Bosque.

---

[74] Webster, p. 162.

Bibliography

Agurcia, Ricardo: Copan, Kingdom Of The Sun.
Asociacion Copan 2007.

Bell, Ellen et al.:   Understanding Early Classic Copan.
University of Pennsylvania Museum of Archeology and
Anthropology 2004.

Braswell, Geoffrey, ed.:   The Maya And Teotihuacan.
University of Texas Press 2003.

Copan Note 3: The Chronology of Altar U

Copan Note 5: Paraphrase of the Text of Altar U

Copan Note 20: The Brother of Yax Pac

Copan Note 23: The Date on the Bench from Structure 9N-
82, Sepulturas, Copan

Copan Note 31: The Inscription on Stela 5 and its Altar

Copan Note 70:   The Early Classic Dynastic History of
Copan

Copan Note 72: Preliminary Commentary on a New Altar
from Structure 30

Copan Note 77: Brothers and Others: New Insights from
the "New Incensarios"

Copan Note 89: Commentary on Altar G

Copan Note 98:   A Commentary on the Inscriptions of
Structure 22A at Copan

Morley, Sylvanus: The Inscriptions At Copan. Originally published by the Carnegie Institution of Washington DC in 1920. This reprint is by Martino Publishing, 2007.

Schele, Linda: A Forest Of Kings. Morrow, 1990.

Stephens, John: Incidents Of Travel In Central America, Chiapas, And Yucatan. Originally published in 1841 by Harper & Brothers. This reprint is by Dover 1969.

Van Cleve, Janice: Who Was Eighteen Rabbit? 2007.

Van Cleve, Janice: Eighteen Rabbit – The Intimate Life And Tragic Death Of A Maya God-King. Originally published by Xlibris 2006. Second edition is by CreateSpace 2013.

Van Cleve, Janice: The Founder – The Life of Yax Kuk Mo, Mover And Shaker In The Maya World. Originally published by Xlibris 2010. This reprint by CreateSpace 2013.

www.mesoweb.com

www.papacweb.org

Webster, David; Freter, Ann Corinne; Gonlin, Nancy: Copan, The Rise And Fall Of An Ancient Maya Kingdom. Wadsworth 2000.

TIKAL'S "BALLCOURT MARKER"

<u>Discovery</u>

The so-called Tikal Ballcourt Marker was discovered by Juan Pedro LaPorte in 1987-1988 in a compound dubbed 6C-XVI by archeologists. This compound is located less than a kilometer south of the Mundo Perdido complex at Tikal. Founded about 250 CE by a clan chief – at the same time as one of Tikal's early kings was refurbishing the Mundo Perdido complex in Teotihuacano style[75] – 6C-XVI went through many stages of rebuilding.

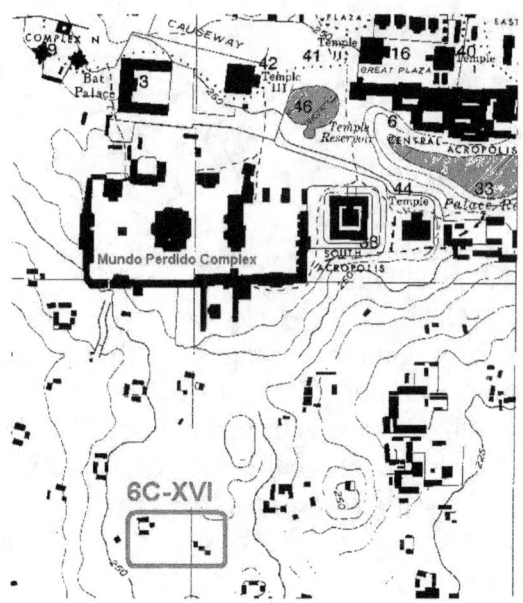

---

[75] Freidel p. 470

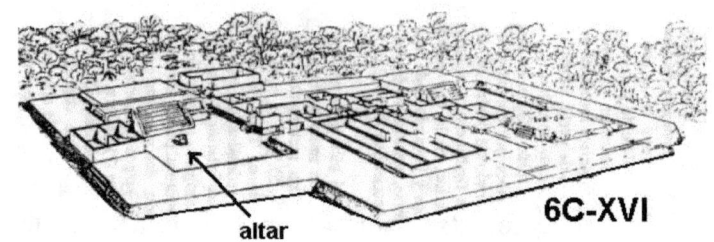

altar

6C-XVI

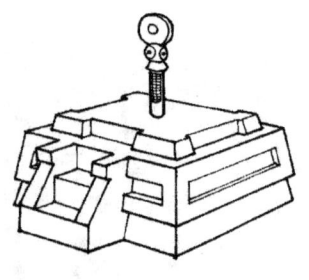

In the first stage, a small shrine in the shape of an open sided stone box was set up in the middle of the north patio. It was remodeled later into a *talud-tablero* altar atop which the ballcourt marker was installed in 414 CE. During the twelfth reconstruction stage[76] this altar was decommissioned around 450-460 CE. Before covering the altar and the whole patio with a new floor, the clan chief of 6C-XVI took down the ballcourt marker and buried it inside the altar with some other offerings. By the time Tikal was abandoned, 6C-XVI supported only a few late architectural features.

---

[76] LaPorte in Braswell pp. 211-212

LaPorte excavated three miles of tunnels underneath the patios in the course of which he discovered the altar and its offerings.

Description

The ballcourt marker stands about three feet tall and is now housed in the National Museum of Archeology and Ethnology in Guatemala City. It is a thick limestone cylinder topped by an oval which is carved on both sides in a ring of feathers. In the center of the feathers on the front is representation of Tlaloc, the rain/lightning god who also symbolized the Teotihuacano style and iconology of war. In the center of the feathers on the back of the oval is an owl and a spearthrower. Below the owl are two heads with non-Maya headdresses and butterfly nose ornaments, typical of Teotihuacan. Below them is a double trapezoid sign wrapped in a cloth. LaPorte suggests the latter may be a Mexican year sign.

However, it could represent a pyramid temple wrapped in the headband of kingship. If subsequent to the Entrada of 378 CE, the ultimate source of royal authority in the Maya world was Teotihuacan, then it would not be much of a stretch to suggest that this wrapped symbol is in fact the *wi-ti-na* mentioned on Tikal stela 31 and elsewhere. On either side of the cylinder shaft are texts.

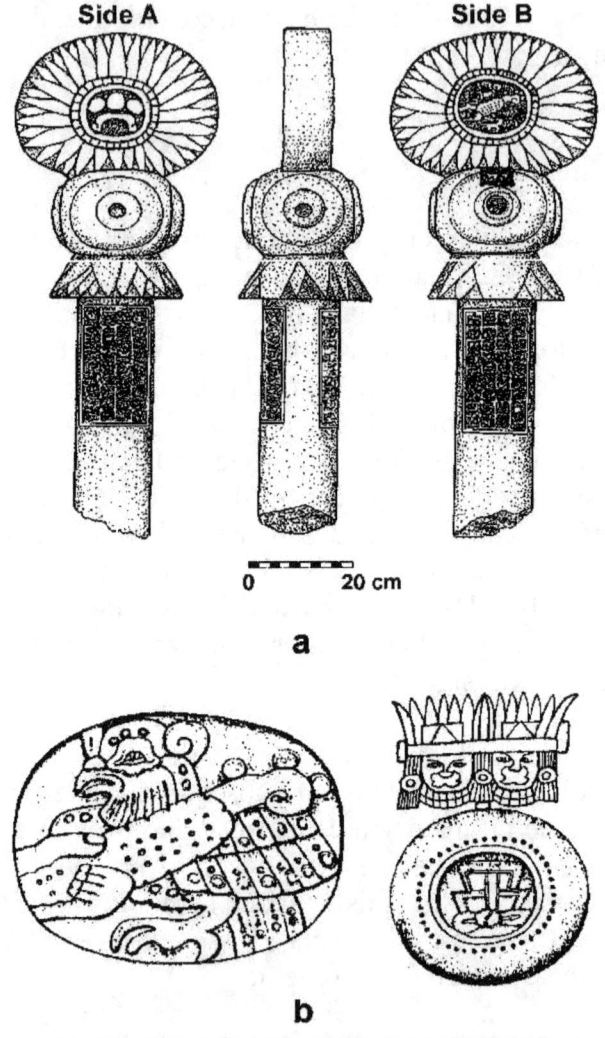

FIGURE 7.6. The Tikal marker, recovered from Group 6C-XVI: (a) three views of marker; (b) details of elements on Side B.

Drawing from Braswell, p. 213

The Text

The inscription on the Tikal marker is Early Classic which retains more logograms in its text than was the case in Middle Classic writing and it still has usages that had fallen away by the height of the Middle Classic. Therefore the glyphs present more challenges than usual. My translation here is very rough. I am indebted to John Montgomery's Dictionary of Maya Hieroglyphs for most of it. Special thanks also to Mark Van Stone, co-author with Michael Coe of Reading The Maya Glyphs, for his notes from David Stuart's 2013 workshop in Antigua. These notes were of great help, as much to unravel some of the glyphs as to highlight the difficulty of others. Finally there were the interpretations by David Freidel in Maya Cosmos and Linda Schele in Forest Of Kings which cast their own instructive light.

Front text of the Tikal Marker

translation	explanation
A1 ISIG	Initial Series indicator for the beginning of a Long Count date.
B1 8 baktuns	
A2 17 katuns	Head variant for 17 without the usual bar-dot notation.
B2 1 tun	
A3 4 winals	
B3 12 kins	B1 – B3 converts to January 13, 378 CE, the date of the great Entrada, the invasion of Tikal by the Teotihuanaco army lead by Siyaj Kak.
A4 the second Lord of the Night was in office	
B4 11 Eb	*haab* calendar.
A5 15 Mac	*tzolkin* calendar. The scribe made an error here, carving two bars = 10 instead of three bars = 15. The math confirms it should be 15.
B5 It was 28 days	
A6 since	bracelet hand in hand is some variant of *k'ab-k'ab* but Schele translates it "since" which makes sense in this context.
B6 it manifested	
A7 the first moon	It was 28 days since the new moon appeared. The Maya were (and are still) very careful to position themselves precisely in time and space.
B7 when he arrived	This is the Old God used as a head variant for *jul-ye-jul-iiy*.
A8 Siyaj Kak	
B8 commander	*kaloomte* is a military title resembling the Roman "imperator"

	or the American "commander-in-chief". It is the title of a war leader who ranks above kings.
A9 its ? place	This may be a particular structure within Tikal. At this date (414), the Mundo Perdido area was the oldest center in the city and was the burial place for Chak Tok Ichaak, the king Siyaj Kak killed when he invaded Tikal.
B9 the Tikal sky cave	References to "sky" in Maya often include the number four as in "4 skies" or the center of the four cardinal directions. The cave is the portal between the worlds for connection to the ancestors. So the "sky cave" could be the central sanctuary of Tikal.
C1 The next day	The *akbal-kin* is "a night and a day" but might be a euphemism for "Next" or "Then".
D1 he arrived	
C2 at the cauac sky shell place	Not sure what this location is but given the context below, it might be the tabernacle where the Tikal god images were housed.
D2 the brother of	*yi-ta* has long been translated as "sibling". Montgomery says it is a relationship glyph meaning "companion of" or "with". Schele writes it *ihtan* and calls it "sibling". Stuart at first proposed "sibling" for this glyph in a letter to Schele in 1988 (Schele, p. 449, footnote 55),

but in Van Stone's notes, Stuart backed away from this definition.

C3 Spearthrower Owl There is much controversy over where this king ruled but the dominant view is that he was the king of Teotihuacan who sent Siyaj Kak to seize Tikal. After Siyaj Kak killed the reigning king of Tikal, he installed Spearthrower's young son, Nuun Ayiin, on the throne. Both Schele (Schele, p. 157) and Freidel (Freidel, p. 296) erroneously call Siyaj Kak the brother of the Tikal king.

D3 ? north completed? This glyph is a mystery.

C4 ? closed the capstone or lid? Stuart in Van Stone's notes suggested "taking something in both hands" but he could not confirm it.

D4 Siyaj Kak He is the actual subject of this whole sentence.

C5 ? A deity?

D5 ? Same or related deity?

C6 he overthrew

D6 ? Unknown sign

C7 sky place? a temple name? Is what we have here is that Siyaj Kak entered a sacred tabernacle and overthrew the gods there, perhaps burning their images? This was a feature of the new style of warfare brought to play by Siyaj Kak; not merely taking captives for sacrifice but actually taking over a place and destroying its sacred and ancestral roots.

D7 the godly place   Referring to the temple?

C8 from the west came

D8 18 images of the war serpent The *waxaklajun ubah chan* is the battle standard or war spirit of the Tlaloc style of warfare.

C9 day god

D9 night god   Stuart says these glyphs are associated with arrival events, perhaps closing the action of this sentence: "And that was the morning and the evening of the next day."

Back text of the Tikal Marker

translation	explanation
E1 11?	Eleven something. Not enough to construct a date.
F1 12 kins, 13 winals, 3 haabs	Three years, thirteen months, and 12 days ago = roughly 1,367 days or April 16, 374.
E2 He acceded	Coronation among the Maya was accomplished by wrapping a band of cloth or paper around the king's head. The literal translation is "wrapping the headband."
F2 to overlordship	
E3 ?	Unknown glyph.
F3 ?	Unknown glyph. In Van Stone's notes Stuart says these two glyphs refer to Spearthrower Owl. Indeed Spearthrower Owl did rise to kingship in 374, although Martin & Grube put the date at May 4, 374.
E4 the five mountains	Could this be a name for Teotihuacan, backed as it was in the Valley of Mexico by high peaks?
F4 high commander of	
E5 the fourth successor	Rephrasing E1-E5: "Spearthrower Owl rose to kingship as the fourth high commander of the 5 mountain place." However, Freidel (Freidel, p.470, footnote 9, suggests that this succession refers to the lineage head of the 6C-XVI compound where his son, Ch'amak, commissioned this ballcourt marker.)
F5 12 muluk	
E6 9 winals? 12 kankin	36 years after the invasion of 378, that is, on January 22, 414.

F6 moon cycle? 15 days ago the lunar month arrived (according to Stuart in Van Stone's notes.)

E7 11 days, 3 winals, 2 tuns, k'al tun 2 years and 71 days before the end of the katun which would occur on March 23, 416. So the inscription not only defines the time since the invasion but also the time before the next 20 year ending cycle.

F7 and then 10 days later

E8 he planted upright

F8 the Tlaloc war banner This is a good example of a logogram instead of syllables. This is an image of the Tlaloc rain/lighting god of Teotihuacan who is the symbol of the new style of warfare brought by Siyaj Kak. Tlaloc emblems were worn on shields and banners – in fact the backside of the feathered disk on this Tikal marker repeats this same symbol. A stone war banner in Teotihuacan bears the same symbol in the center of its feathered disk. (see below)

E9 of Spearthrower

F9 Owl Owner of the Tikal Ballcourt Marker/war banner.

G1 He did it This refers to the lord who actually commissioned this ballcourt marker. He is not Spearthrower Owl, Siyaj Kak, nor Nuun Ayiin.

H1 the banner stone lord Excellent example of a logogram. H1a is an actual representation of this ballcourt

		marker in place atop its altar. H1b is "ahau" or lord.
G2	properly	In the right order, as "according to the accepted norms" or "following in the footsteps of"
H2	on his land	
G3	?	Unknown glyph, possibly a title.
H3	Ch'amak?	This is possibly the name of the lord who commissioned this ballcourt marker. Freidel (Freidel pp. 299-300) came up with this name.
G4	a lord of	Ch'amak is a vassal of Siyaj Kak. Perhaps he is even the lineage head of the clan that lives in 6C-XVI?
H4	Siyaj Kak	
G5	like when he arrived	When Siyaj Kak arrived . .
H5	at the Tikal portal	
G6	from the 5 mountain valley	
H6	with [the banner of] the 18 images	
G7	of the turquoise serpent	
H7	It was taken	
G8	from the zero first god?	Is this a place or a person?
H8	Spearthrower + toast with wings?	
G9	?	Unknown glyphs
H9	Spearthrower Owl lord	

Ballcourt Marker or War Banner?

LaPorte makes a case that this Tikal artifact is a ballcourt marker and this attribution has remained in the literature since his report. He bases his case on the fact that he found no elements of residence, kinship, or production at 6C-XVI[77].
He found no evidence of densely populated apartments, nor many hearths or middens, and only a few burials. Although there are no ballcourts in 6C-XVI, LaPorte notes that two murals depict ball players. LaPorte suggested that 6C-XVI may have been a kind of Spartan academy for ballplayers.

Schele expanded on LaPorte's thesis[78]. She noted that a very similar artifact was found at La Ventilla complex at Teotihuacan. Note in the illustration that it has the same Tlaloc image in the center of a feathered disk as the Tikal marker.

---

[77] LaPorte in Braswell, p. 210
[78] Schele, pp. 158 and 451

Another artifact from Kaminaljuyu which is often cited as a ballcourt marker similar to the Teotihuacano and Tikal examples bears no resemblance to either (see illustration)/

While Maya ballcourt markers typically were round disks planted in the floor of the ball court, Schele pointed to a different kind of game played with sticks which did appear to include upright markers. The Mural of Tepantitla is one example. Another, identified by Koontz (p. 22) shows a similar marker and a scattering of players with sticks and balls.

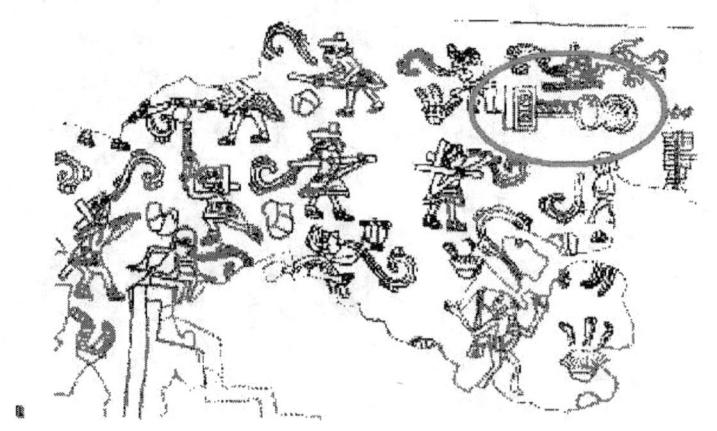

Freidel noted, however, that these "ballcourt markers" were actually stone representations of battle standards which may on occasion have been placed at some ballcourts as trophies, not of game victories, but of war victories[79]. He says "we think this effigy is a copy of a standard originally carried by Ch'amak's predecessor into battle alongside his war leader, Smoking Frog" (Siyaj Kak)[80]. The text itself names the Tikal marker as the Tlaloc war banner of Spearthrower Owl. Examples of just such war banners are vividly displayed in the famous murals of Bonampak (drawing courtesy of FAMSI). Therefore it would be more correct to refer to this artifact at Tikal as the Tikal War Banner effigy.

---

[79] Freidel, p. 470 footnote 8
[80] Friedel, p. 299

The author, Janice Van Cleve, in the National Museum in Guatelmala City with the Tikal War Banner.

Bibliography

Bernal, Ignacio: 100 Masterpieces of the Mexican National Museum of Anthropology. New York 1969. #8

Braswell, Geoffrey ed.: The Maya And Teotihuacan. University of Texas Press, Austin 2003.

Brown, Kathryn and Stanton, Travis eds.: Ancient Mesoamerican Warfare. Altamira 2003.

Fialko, Vilma: El Marcador de Juego de Pelota de Tikal 1988 in Primer Symposio Mundial Sobre Epigrafia Maya, pp 61-80. Guatemala City, Asociation Tikal.

Foundation for the Advancement of Mesoamerican Studies, www.famsi.org.

Freidel, David; Schele, Linda; Parker, Joy: Maya Cosmos. Harper Collins, New York 1993. 468-473, 293-326

Koontz, Rex: Lightning Gods And Feathered Serpents: The Public Sculpture Of El Tajin. University of Texas Press, Austin. 2010.

LaPorte, Juan Pedro: Alternativas del Clasico Temprano en la relacion Tikal-Teotihuacan: Grupo 6C-XVI. 1988. A Dissertation for a Doctoral en Antropologia, Universidad Nacional Automona de Mexico.

LaPorte, Juan Pedro: El Grupo 6C-XVI, Tikal, Peten: Un centro habitacional del Classico Temprano. 1987. Memorias del I Coloquio International del Mayastas, Centro de Estudios Mayas, pp. 221-244, Universidad Nacional Automona de Mexico.

LaPorte, Juan Pedro: Architectural Aspects of Interaction Between Tikal and Teotihuacan during the Early Classic Period. In The Maya and Teotihuacan edited by Geoffrey Braswell, 2009.

Martin, Simon and Grube, Nikolai: Chronicle of Maya Kings & Queens. Thames & Hudson, London 2000.

Montgomery, John: Dictionary of Maya Hieroglyphs. New York 2002.

Schele, Linda and Freidel, David: A Forest Of Kings. Morrow, New York 1990.

Valdes, Juan Antonio: Los Mascarones del Grupo 6C-XVI de Tikal in Estudios de Cultura Maya vol XVIII, 1991.

Van Stone, Mark: Personal notes from David Stuart's presentation in Antigua, 2013.

COPAN'S PECCARY SKULL

Discovery

The famous inscribed peccary skull from Copan could be one of the most important pieces in the puzzle of the life of Yax Kuk Mo, founder of the Copan dynasty. Diana Fridberg's 2005 Harvard University thesis entitled "Peccaries in Ancient Maya Economy, Ideology, and Iconography" is the best and most detailed analysis of peccaries in general and of this skull in particular. This paper is indeed indebted to her work, but the focus here is on the interpretation of the cartouche carved in the center of the skull.

Tomb 1 excavation. Photo by Marshall Saville, 1892

There are actually two peccary skulls. Both were discovered just south of the main acropolis in Tomb 1 excavated by Marshall Saville in 1892. He and John Owens found a number of burials in this area which inspired locals to name it El Cementerio, even though it was not per se an official Maya cemetery. (Owens later died while working at Copan and was buried at the north end of the Great Plaza in front of stela D[81]).

Tomb 1 is located under the foundations of a structure numbered 10L-236 by archeologists[82] (see map in appendix A). It is an elaborate masonry tomb, containing two chambers with the remains of two adults[83]. The tomb dates from around 600-650 CE[84], during the beginning of the reign of Smoke Jaguar. This was evidently an elite burial on the basis of the quality of the items buried with them including a dog's head effigy vessel and other ceramic vessels, modified and unmodified animal bones, obsidian, jadeite, ochre, and shell.

The tomb also included broken pieces of two inscribed peccary skulls. Saville recorded their finding:

"Near the corner B. on the stone floor were found two skulls of someanimal. These were broken in a number of

---

[81] Barbara Fash personal communication. See also Morley, p. 84.

[82] Andrews, p. 249.

[83] PAPAC (Proyecto Arqueologico para la Planificacion de la Antigua Copan) identifies another tomb 1 in the Bosque complex which contained remains of only one adult.

[84] Fridberg, p. 40.

pieces. Number one was nearest the southern wall, with the top of the skull on the stone floor. The other was with the top of the skull up, and close to no. 1. This was more destroyed than the first one but had some very fine hieroglyphs carved onit. They were carved and evidently intended for vessels (Saville 1892:34)"[85].

Both are currently in the Peabody Museum.

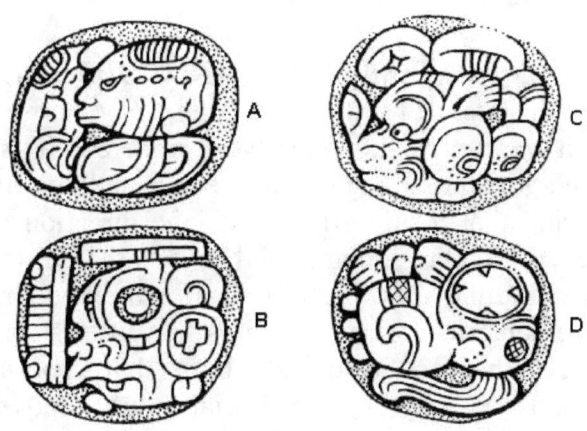

Peccary Skull 2

Peccary Skull 2 has been reassembled since Fridberg wrote her thesis. The skull has four glyphs, two on each side. The first two, A-B, read: u-ba-ki AJ-?-NAAH which translates "It is the bone of the one from big eye house". Zender notes that B contains a rare fish sign with a large eye[86]. This place name also occurs on Smoke Jaguar's

[85] Fridberg, p. 40.
[86] Zender, no page.

stela 12 (F9). This might relate to the water management clans proposed by Barbara Fash[87]. She argues that the social organization of Copan was based on clans, one of whose chief duties was the management of water resources. The "fish" clan is identified with the Cementerio area of Copan and Tomb 1 is in the same area. The clan, represented on the *Popol Nah* council house by a fish symbol, was based south of the acropolis, exactly where Tomb 1 is located. Peccary Skull 2 demonstrates that the "fish" clan was already established in that part of Copan as early as 600-650.

Glyphs C-D read: *xuk-pi-AJAW NOJ-OHL (Y)OON?-ni* which translates "Lord of Copan, Southern Yoon". Although *yoon-ni* is not clearly deciphered, it is a title connected to Smoke Jaguar on stela 6 and on altar K[88]. Considering that it is prefixed with the direction of south and the "fish" clan's compound is located south of the acropolis, and the 16th king of Copan, who made his home in the Cementerio area, also claims this title (stela 29 and temple 21A bench), it strongly hints that *yoon-ni* could mean "clan", "family", or "territorial unit." Smoke Jaguar and his later successor, the 16th king, are iconographically claiming membership in the "fish" clan.

Smoke Jaguar was buried in the Chorka Tomb underneath temple 26, which obviously means that Tomb 1 does not contain his remains. Therefore Peccary Skull 2 could have been a prized gift from that king to the person buried with it. Given the other elite gifts in Tomb 1, the person buried

---

[87] Fash in Andrews, pp. 103-138.
[88] Zender, no page. Stela 6 is located between the Principle Group and the modern village. Altar K was found in the middle court at the north end of 10L-6.

next to corner B may have been a member of the royal family.

<u>Peccary Skull 1</u>

Intriguing as Peccary Skull 2 is, it is Peccary Skull 1 which has excited the most attention (illustration originally from Fash, William: <u>Scribes, Warriors and Kings</u>. Thames & Hudson 1992).

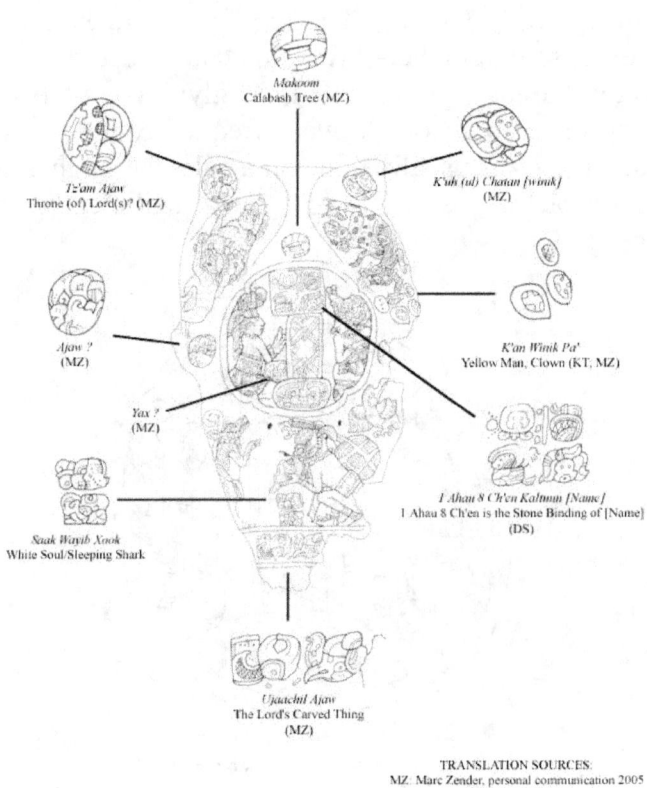

Makoom
Calabash Tree (MZ)

Tz'am Ajaw
Throne (of) Lord(s)? (MZ)

K'uh (ul) Chanan [winik]
(MZ)

Ajaw ?
(MZ)

K'an Winik Pa'
Yellow Man, Clown (KT, MZ)

Yax ?
(MZ)

I Ahau 8 Ch'en Kaltuun [Name]
1 Ahau 8 Ch'en is the Stone Binding of [Name]
(DS)

Saak Wayib Xook
White Soul/Sleeping Shark

Ujaachil Ajaw
The Lord's Carved Thing
(MZ)

TRANSLATION SOURCES:
MZ: Marc Zender, personal communication 2005
DS: Stuart 1996
KT: Taube 1989

Our attention is drawn to the central cartouche in which we see two individuals sitting on either side of a wrapped stela and altar. Above the altar is a block of four glyphs. The inscription reads *hun ahau waxak chen kaltuun foliated ahau*, which translates "On 1 Ahau 8 Chen is the stone binding of Foliated Ahau." The date has long been attached to long count 8.17.0.0.0[89] which converts to October 19, 376. There are eight dates within the 8th baktun which could fit 1 Ahau 8 Chen – in CE 65, 116, 168, 220, 272, 324, 376, and 428. Most of these are very early for an historical event at Copan but the last two are possible. Only October 19, 376 falls on a katun ending, however, so epigraphers favor this date because of the third glyph in the inscription. The third glyph is a verb meaning to bind or wrap a stone, a word frequently used to set up a stela, which was usually done on a calendar ending date. In fact the picture itself shows a very deliberately wrapped stela.

Central medallion of the peccary skull
(drawing by Barbara W. Fash)

---

[89] See Bell, <u>Understanding Early Classic Copan</u>, p. 223 and Schele, Copan Note #96, p. 3 and Fridberg, p. 51.

The fourth glyph is the famous "Foliated Ahau." This glyph appears on Copan stela I, Copan stela 4, and Pusilha stela K, all referencing the same katun ending 8.6.0.0.0 – 10 Ahau 13 Chen or December 16, 159[90]. From Uaxactun there is a bowl with the portraits of four lords, one of whom has what appears to be a Foliated Ahau in his headdress.[91] I found a Maya vase up for auction[92] which claims to have a Foliated Ahau glyph on the upraised tail of a jaguar and there is another Foliated Ahau glyph on a jade pendant from Costa Rica. The latter two are undated and I have not examined them myself. Finally, there is a Foliated Ahau Balam Kaloomte on the back of Tikal stela 31 (glyph blocks C5-D5) who appears in the list of kings for that city around the time of 159 CE.[93] If Foliated Ahau is the name of a person, he certainly covered a lot of ground all in the same year!

Copan stela I - foliated ahau

Copan stela 4 - foliated ahau

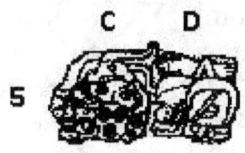

Tikal stela 31
foliated ahau

Schele and Newsome put forth the opinion that "foliated ahau" is not the name of a person at all but is instead a rank

---

[90] Copan stela 17 also references the date 8.6.0.0.0. Unfortunately it is broken and nothing more can be read. Schele, Copan Note #30.

[91] Boot, p. 18.

[92] It was for sale from Artifact Premium (www.artfact.com) during the last week of December 2008.

[93] Martin & Grube, p. 27.

or title.[94] They translate the glyph as *ya-nik-hun* which is a flowered or white headband. The taking of the flowered headband is equivalent to the taking of a crown as in the coronation of a king in medieval Europe. So alluding to someone as the "Flowered Headband Lord" is equivalent to calling him "His Majesty". In the scene on Peccary Skull 1, the lord sitting on the right hand side, which is the superior position, is also facing front, which denotes the highest ranking person. Schele and Newsome conclude, therefore, that he is the owner of the flowered or white headband and by extension, he is the king who wrapped the stela and marked the katun in 376. The translation of the brief inscription should thus read: "On 1 Ahau 8 Chen he wrapped up the katun, he of the flowered headband."

Who is this Flowered Headband Lord? The Maya frequently alluded to the identity of their portraits in the headdresses. The lord on the left of the peccary skull is certainly Yax Kuk Mo as he bears a quetzal macaw for a headdress[95]. If this is the case, then the lord on the right should likewise be identified by his headdress. David Stuart calls it a jaguar[96] but the only kings around in 376 with "jaguar" in their names are at Yaxchitlan and there are no obvious ties between that city and Copan[97]. The headdress looks more like a crocodile or curl nosed monster to me, and there is a king in Tikal named Yax Nuun Ayiin I who fits the time period. His name translates First or Green Crocodile (nicknamed by archeologists "Curl Snout"). He was installed as king of Tikal by Mexican general Siyaj Kak in 378 and he died in 404.

---

[94] Schele, Copan Note Nr. 96.
[95] He also favors his right arm and gestures with his left and has a *yax* bundle in his lap.
[96] Bell, Understanding Early Classic Copan, p. 223.
[97] Martin & Grube, p. 21.

If indeed Nuun Ayiin is the Flowered Headband Lord on the peccary skull, then this inscription may show evidence of a very important moment in the life of Yax Kuk Mo. By sitting in the subordinate position and pointing to the text that may designate Nuun Ayiin as a king, Yax Kuk Mo would be acknowledging the authority of Nuun Ayiin over himself. However, by all accounts, Nuun Ayiin was only a young child in 376[98]. He was only installed as king of Tikal in 378 under the authority of his uncle, Siyaj Kak. It is therefore not likely that Nuun Ayiin could perform a kingly act like raising a stela at the end a katun before he was installed as king.

Moreover, Yax Kuk Mo died in 437. If the scene on the Peccary Skull 1 is intended to show an actual historical event, with both of these men present as adults (at least 20 years of age), then Yax Kuk Mo would have had to live at minimum 81 years. This is impressive, but not impossible[99]. According to Altar Q, he journeyed from "the Root Tree House" to Copan in 426. This took him 153 days and, if he was 20 years old in 376, he would have accomplished this impressive feat when he was 70! He could have been carried in a palanquin, to be sure, but again this is stretching the limits of human endurance. Moreover, he had suffered many injuries during his lifetime, some of which had not healed.

---

[98] Martin & Grube, p. 33 and Braswell, p. 24.

[99] By the same calculations, Nuun Ayiin would have been at least 48 when he died in 404 – a perfectly reasonable, if young, age.

 Foliated Jester God sculpture from Altun Ha

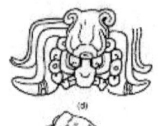 Foliated Jester God atop Copan stela P

 Maize God as Foliated Jester God. Note ahau glyph atop his head.

 Foliated Jester God atop Pax God pectoral.

 Maize God wearing headdress of foliated Jester God from Copan, an offering.

Images and notes from Karl Taube in
"The Symbolism of Jade in Classic Maya Religion

It is more plausible that the scene on Peccary Skull 1 is not representing an actual historical event but a supernatural one. After all, the entire skull depicts scenes from the Otherworld with a quatrefoil portal open to view the two lords in the mundane world. It could be that Yax Kuk Mo was not present at the actual wrapping of the katun, but he is alluding to it after the fact. The child Nuun Ayiin may also not have been present at the katun wrapping and in any event he was still in Teotihuacan in 376.

Who then is "Foliated Ahau"? Karl Taube has shown that the Jester God is often depicted as a Foliated Ahau.

The "foliage" comes from the leaves of the maize plant, which was the staple food of Mesoamerican peoples. The identification of rulership and sustenance originated with the Olmecs[100] and became a key symbol of kingship among the Maya.

It seems certain, therefore, that Foliated Ahau is not a personal name, but a title. That this title appears in so many places in early Maya history or at least in reference to early Maya history, may be due to closer temporal proximity to the Olmec culture that preceded the Maya. Another possibility is that as kingship matured in the Maya region, newer titles replaced the more archaic Foliated Ahau title.

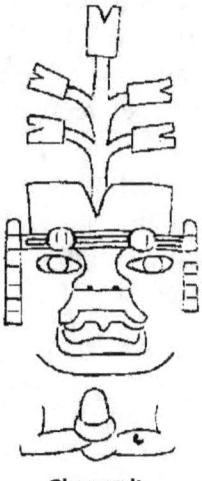

Olmec celt

Conclusion

On Peccary Skull 1, Yax Kuk Mo is referring retrospectively to the end of a katun celebrated by "His Majesty" while Nuun Ayinn looks on. The only "majesty" that both men would recognize would be the emperor of Teotihuacan. Yax Kuk Mo went to Teotihuacan to gain his regalia of kingship before marching to Copan and Nuun Ayiin was the son of the emperor and was installed as king of Tikal by his uncle, the emperor's brother. Spearthrower Owl assumed the emperor's throne of Teotihuacan in 374, so he was in place to wrap the katun in 376[101]. He died in

[100] Fields, The Iconographic Heritage of the Maya Jester God in www.mesoweb.com. 1991.

439 according to Tikal stela 31. His life spanned the lives of both Yax Kuk Mo and Nuun Ayiin and it was from him that both received their authority to rule. It is likely, therefore, that the majesty to which Yax Kuk Mo refers on Peccary Skull 1 is Spearthrower Owl.

The peccary skulls were carved early in the reign of Smoke Jaguar (628-695). He was a 5 katun lord, well into his 80's, when he died and therefore must have been born sometime between 606 and 614. He would have been young when he assumed the throne. The carving on Peccary Skull 1 may have been intended to show that his lineage – and therefore legitimacy to rule – harked all the way back through the founder of his dynasty all the way to Teotihuacan itself.

---

[101] Stelae were not a feature of Teotihuacano political or religious life. The carver of Peccary Skull 1 was however

Appendix A

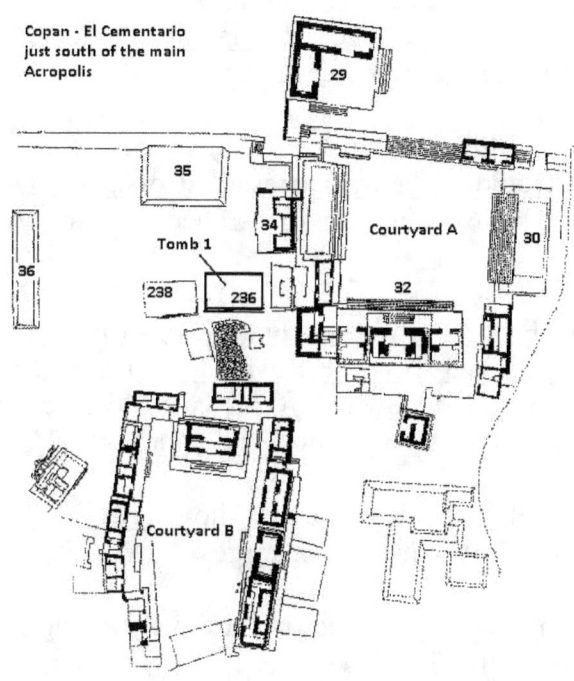

Copan - El Cementario
just south of the main
Acropolis

29

35

34

Tomb 1

Courtyard A

30

36

238   236

32

Courtyard B

Site of Tomb 1 today. Photo by author.

Bibliography

Andrews, E. Wyllys and Fash, William, eds.: Copan. The History Of An Ancient Maya Kingdom. School of American Research Press 2005.

Bell, Ellen; Canuto, Marcello; Sharer, Robert: Understanding Early Classic Copan. University of Pennsylvania Museum of Archeology and Anthropology 2004.

Boot, Erik: Portraits of Four Kings of the Early Classic? An Inscribed Bowl Excavated at Uaxactun and Seven Vessels of Unknown Provenance. Mesoweb Publications, www.mesoweb.com/articles/boot/UaxactunBowl.pdf.

Braswell, Geoffrey, ed.: The Maya and Teotihuacan. Austin, University of Texas Press 2003.

Copan Note #30 "Stela I and the Founding of the City of Copan" – 1987. Linda Schele.

Copan Note #96 "Taking the Headband at Copan" – 1991. Linda Schele and Elizabeth Newsome.

Copan Note #122 "The Tikal-Copan Connection, version 2." – 1993. Linda Schele, Nikolai Grube, Fredrico Fahsen.

Fields, Virginia: The Iconographic Heritage of the Maya Jester God in www.mesoweb.com.

Fridberg, Diana: "Peccaries in Ancient Maya Economy, Ideology, and Iconography" Harvard University thesis 2005.

Martin, Simon and Grube Nicolai: Chronicle Of The Maya Kings And Queens. Thames & Hudson 2000.

Montgomery, John: Dictionary Of Maya Hieroglyphs. Hippocrene Books 2002.

Morley, Sylvanus: An Introduction To The Study Of The Maya Hieroglyphs. Dover 1975.

Taube, Karl: "The Symbolism of Jade In Classic Maya Religion"   Ancient   Mesoamerica   #16   2005. www.academia.edu.

Van Cleve, Janice: The Founder. The Life Of Yax Kuk Mo, Mover And Shaker In The Maya World. CreateSpace 2013.

Zender, Marc: "Peccary Skull No. 2, Tomb 1, Copan, Honduras & A Report on the New Peccary Skull Glyphs" Peabody Museum 2009. www.academia.edu.

MODERN MAYA RITUALS

By great good fortune I was invited to join a tour through Guatemala as a guest lecturer in 2010. The major focus of our itinerary was to witness and participate in a number of modern Maya rituals.

The Maya developed a very sophisticated civilization which flourished in Central America for almost 1,500 years – from 250 BCE to the Spanish Conquest in the 16th Century. The classic period of Maya history when they build their most famous temples and cities was between 250 and 900 CE. They mysteriously abandoned their southern cities to the jungle in the 9th Century which is fortunate for archeologists because, unlike Athens or Rome, these ruins were not recycled into later cities. Except for the impacts of weather, roots, and time, they are very much as the Maya left them.

Today the lands of Yucatan, Chiapas, Guatemala, Belize, Honduras, and El Salvador are home to some seven million Maya. Lands communally held by native farmers in ancient times were gobbled up by the Spanish during the conquest and the Maya were forced to work in near slavery for their new masters. That pattern has continued in modern times in which the Ladino urban elite have dominated politics and the economy at the expense of the rural Maya. But the Maya have often rebelled. The whole second half of the 19th Century saw the Maya almost succeed in overthrowing Mexican control of the Yucatan. There were rebellions in the 20th Century in El Salvador and Chiapas, sparking a sanctuary movement in the United

States for refugees of the conflicts. Guatemala convulsed in a bloody civil war that ended only in 1996.

The peace treaty ending that war allowed the Maya, among other things, to practice their religion again. A visitor to Tikal or one of the many other sites in Guatemala today may be surprised to see new altars in the old ruins blackened by recent sacrificial fires. Some of those sacrificial fires were burned by us on our trip to see and participate in modern Maya rituals.

Eight Batz Ritual

Momostenango lies in the heart of Quiche country. The Quiche Maya live in the rich fertile highlands of western Guatemala where they grow maize, vegetables, and beans just like their ancestors did 2000 years ago. And just like their ancestors, they mark the turning of the 260 day *tzolkin* calendar in a ceremony called Eight Batz. Eight Batz is the beginning of the next 260 day ritual cycle. The Maya also follow the annual *haab* calendar of 18 months of 20 days each and one unlucky month of 5 days duration. Still another calendar called the Long Count tracks the number of days since the Fourth Creation. This is the one that begins the inscriptions on most of the classical dated monuments. It is the Long Count calendar that turned over on December 21, 2012. The Maya don't use this calendar anymore and could care less about the so-called end of the world that fascinates some non-Maya groups in the United States.

We gather on a hilltop outside of the city. This is one of five or six hilltops on which worshippers are coming together to burn offerings and make their petitions to the gods for the coming cycle. It is 4:00 am and pitch dark. The stars shine brightly overhead. We easily pick out the turtle constellation which is how the Maya classify Orion's belt. We see the triangle of the three stars – Alnitak, Rigel, and Saiph – which form the hearthstone or place of origin for the Maya. They believe that this is where creation began.

The shaman prepares the fire very carefully. First he makes a circle of sugar about three feet in diameter. He quarters the circle with sugar and makes a small circle in each of the quarters. Then he places a ring of copal incense nodules around the outer rim and four large cones of copal in the center. The space between the cones he fills with charcoal. Atop that he carefully arranges a pyramid of sticks, herbs, and cigars. He alternates thin taper candles around the top – white for the ancestors and yellow for healing. Each of us is given two candles of each color which we hold tightly in our hands in anticipation for what follows.

The shaman prays in Quiche. We don't understand what he is saying. We have paid money in advance for this ritual to cover the cost of materials, etc. Since money is an form of energy in our modern society, our contributions help to transform us from being merely spectators to active participants. Our donations are a realistic and efficient way to demonstrate our respect for the shaman who is praying on our behalf and to join our energies with his.

Four other shamans join us. They call the four directions in this order: east then west, north and finally south. East is red for the dawn. West is black for the night. North is white for the clouds and south is yellow for the noonday sun. The shamans do not cast a circle. The hilltop is apparently already holy ground that needs no clearing, casting, or consecrating. When the fire gets going, they invoke each of the 20 day signs in all 13 of their aspects:

one Imix, two Imix, three Imix and so on. Now we are grounded in both space and time. When all 260 days of the cycle have been invoked, the chief shaman invites each of us to put our prayers and wishes into the candles and one by one step up to the fire and throw them in. Fire is the catalyst which converts offerings into smoke which the gods can consume. In classical times they burned blood soaked papers and beating hearts of victims the same way for the same reason.

Every so often the shaman splashes alcohol on each of the four quarters to flare up the flames. He dumps a healthy scoop of granular copal into a charcoal fired censer and walks around behind us liberally bathing us in the sweet smelling incense. Afterwards we approach the fire individually a second time to smudge ourselves. We scoop the smoke over and around our bodies in 13 repetitions. Then the shaman's wife takes a bouquet of flowers and after infusing it with smoke, strokes everyone's aura with it front and back. At the end of the ceremony, there is no devocation of the day signs. Instead, the shamans line up and we pass by them giving each a double hug. The fire is left to burn out of its own accord when we leave.

This same ritual is performed at two other altars on our hilltop and on four other hilltops in the area. Momostenango means "place of many altars". By this time the sun is risen and we can see smoke rising from the other hills. Some shamans and their initiates stay up all night and make a pilgrimage to each of the five hilltops. This ceremony will be repeated after another 260 days have passed.

Maximon Ritual

Santiago lies on the south shore of Lake Atitlan which is itself the deep throat of an a huge ancient volcano filled with water. It has no spillway, but rather empties through cracks in its floor caused by earthquakes centuries ago. Santiago is one of the centers of the Kaqchikel Maya who were a main target of government oppression during the civil war.

The men of Santiago centuries ago created a god they called Maximon. They freely acknowledge that they created him – no star in the east, no divine revelation, no initiated tradition handed down. This is important because it shows that at least in some instances the Maya understand that they have the power to create gods as they need them. In this case, this god was supposed to protect the women of the town while the men were away on business, because Santiago is on the main trade route from communities on the Pacific coast to the highlands.

However, the story goes that the men discovered that their women were getting pregnant anyway and they suspected Maximon. They cut off the idol's arms and legs (and the other appendage) and they converted him into a deity from whom they ask favors. I did not witness any prayers or actions that showed worship of the god for his own sake, at least as far as I could grasp. They appear rather to focus upon him their prayers and supplications. I'm not sure if he is supposed to be an intercessor and to whom, or if they believe he has the power himself to grant their wishes. We learned that they trot him out on parade during Easter week and otherwise house him in a shabby backroom shrine on a side street.

Our path to Maximon seemed at first to have all the earmarks of a scam. First our guide said not everybody can visit Maximon, especially tourists. You have to know where he is (scam sign #1 – create mystery and exclusivity). Then the guide took us on a winding path through the dank warrens of the city to a narrow dim alley (scam sign #2 – take your marks on a journey. This invests them in the mystery). Then just before you go in talk about offerings but be very vague about how much is enough (scam sign #3 – shake down for cash.) By this time the marks will figure "Oh well, we've come this far, we may as well pay." It really wasn't all that much, actually, and it is an effective way of contributing our energy to the ritual.

The shrine is in a dim dusty back room in a rambling barrio of similar rooms. It has a tin roof and no windows. The ceiling is decked out in a checkerboard of cheap plastic doilies interspersed with colored balloons. Two of the checkerboard squares hold circular fluorescent lights for illumination. Leaning against the walls on either side of the entrance are painted statues of saints carved of wood like you'd expect in an old village church. Among them is a statute for death and several images in coffins decked with plastic flowers. Votive lamps flicker before them.

In the center of the room is a table with a bench behind for visitors and the idol of Maximon propped up in front. About 12 votives flicker in front of him. He smokes and drinks so a lighted cigarette is constantly in his mouth. This creates the image of movement and life in the statue. He is clothed with various hanks of cloth and on his head are two cowboy hats, both with pink and purple veils hanging off the back.

On either side of the idol are stools on which sit the acolytes. The one on the left tends the cigarette, occasionally catching the ash in a pan or inserting a new one and lighting it. The one on the right assists the deacon. He counts out the donations very openly as part of the ritual, he keeps the censer burning, and he helps the deacon with communion. Communion, by the way, consists of beer and 150 proof rum. Alcohol is a key ingredient of Maya rituals. Bishop Landa in 1566 noted that the natives got drunk during their religious ceremonies and Evon Vogt noted in his anthropological study (1970) of the Zinacanteco Maya in Chiapas that rum is an essential ingredient of their religious practices.

Then the priest arrives with his client. They kneel before Maximon and line up more candles in front of the votives already there. The priest prays on the client's behalf. The prayers were in Kaqchikel which I did not understand, but they seemed to say that the client is a good person and please grant her request. At one point the priest removes one of the cowboy hats off of the idol and places it on his client's head with the veil hanging down in front covering her face. He says some more prayers and then has her kiss the hat on all four of its sides before returning it to the idol. This may have been a symbolic way of bonding the client and the god.

The acolyte hands the priest a crude censer made out of a large tin can which is filled with burning charcoal. It has a handle fashioned out of a coat hanger. The priest heaps generous scoops of copal into this censer producing thick clouds of sweet smoke. He censes the idol, his client, and himself. Then he passes it around so we can all smudge ourselves. The tightly crowded room, billowing smoke, flickering candles in the dark, and tacky decorations are almost overpowering. Our vision blurs and breathing is difficult. The mind gets a little dizzy. The combination actually does work to transform the dingy little room into an otherworldly place.

Toward the end of the ceremony the client makes her personal prayers to Maximon. She seems not at all shy that she is asking for very personal things in front of all these visitors. In fact our role there lends support to her pleas and she gratefully asks Maximon to include our wishes with her own. Finally the deacon pours the beer and passes the cups around. Then he pours shot glasses of the rum and passes them as well. After he repeats this several times, we're all thinking this religion is looking pretty dang good! The acolytes even tilt back the idol so they can pour beer and rum into his mouth as well. After the first ceremony, a second priest came in with his client and the whole rite was repeated.

Rose Petal Rituals

The end of the civil war in Guatemala not only allowed Maya shamans to construct altars and lead rituals at classical Maya sites. The people themselves gained the right in some cases to preserve and rebuild temples in the ancient cities. What they build may not be archeologically correct, but it is culturally correct and this is what they have

done at Iximche, which is between Lake Atitlan and Antigua. This former Kaqchikel capital rebelled against the Spanish after earlier joining them against their rivals, the Quiche. In one corner of this sprawling complex, the native people have built a small temple with niches on all four sides for votive offerings much like the votive candle racks in Catholic churches. Before this temple is a circular concrete altar where we performed another ritual.

The ritual at Iximche and the one at Quirigua were both led by the same shaman and his family who accompanied us on our journey. The performances were both very similar so I have chosen to combine them here.

The shaman covers the altar with a graceful carpet of pinon fronds. Over this he carefully designs a four pointed star in rose petals creating compass points to each of the four directions. In the center he constructs a circle of copal nodules with a pile of charcoal in the center. On this base he raises a pyramid of wood and colored candles crowned by a spire of candles at the peak.

The candles represent a sacrifice of all that we hold dear, including even our very bodies. Red candles signify blood, the burning of which is food for the gods and a symbolic substitute for a more sanguine offering. White is for bone. Yellow is for flesh. The Maya believe that the Fourth Creation was the fourth attempt by the gods to create worshippers who could articulate prayers and remember the rites. The result of this creation was humans made from maize, hence the yellow color for flesh. Green and blue are merged together to represent Nature. Black is for the night. They use cream colored candles as well, but their significance was not explained. The family's children pass out two candles of each color to each of us – except for the cream colored ones.

Over to the side at the base of the reconstructed pyramid, is laid out the shaman's personal altar. In the center of a circle of beads are two equilateral crosses. These appear to represent the sun (like on the flag for the state of New Mexico in the USA) because where the arms intersect is molded an *ahau* day sign. I did not see if the one underneath had the number of the day, but it would not surprise me. There is a mask of a god above the circle of beads as well.

The shaman calls the four directions in the Maya way: east first, then west, followed by north, then south. He prays to the lord of the day and this time we all kneel and he kisses the altar in a clear sign of worship. His censer is a nice ceramic model with a ceramic handle. With it he censes the altar and then walks around behind each of us to bathe us in smoke. I think the translator said this was part of a purification rite, but I'm not sure I captured that correctly.

Then began the counting of the days. The shaman and his wife alternated chanting the 13 counts of each of the 20 days, occasionally tossing a candle into the fire. Several days before in Antigua we calculated our personal day signs which serve as our zodiac natal signs in Maya terms. According to one source, the Maya count daybreak as the beginning of the new day, not midnight, so since I was born at 1:09 am, my sign is the one from what would correspond to the previous day in Gregorian reckoning. As the count of days proceeds, we listen for our day sign. When we hear it, we step forward, pray our desires into our candles, and toss them into the fire.

The kids come round again and give us each a handful of sesame seeds. When we throw them into the flames it makes a crackling sound. We also throw in handfuls of sugar. The shaman stirs the fire one more time and stokes the censer. He walks around us to smoke us all again and sets the censer on the altar. Then we walk widdershins around the circle, stopping to smudge ourselves in the smoke of the fire and the smoke of the incense. Finally we end the ritual with hugs all around.

Conclusion

There are not many resources for further study of modern Maya ritual practices. Evon Vogt's The Zinacantecos of Mexico: A Modern Maya Way of Life (Holt, Rinehart and Winston 1970) is one of the best scientific anthropological studies. The much better known Maya Cosmos: Three Thousand Years on the Shaman's Path by David Freidel, Linda Schele, and Joy Parker (Harper Collins 1993) is hugely valuable as much for the informed speculations of the authors as for their eyewitness accounts. Of course no understanding of Maya mythology can even begin without the Popol Vuh translated by Dennis Tedlock (Simon & Schuster 1985). This is the Maya bible as it has come down from the Quiche people. There are also nine Chilam Balam books from several Yucatan towns which were compiled in the 18th and 19th centuries which contain prophesies, herbal lore, calendrics, astrology, and mythology. Finally, there is a paper by Nicholas Hopkins and J. Kathryn Josserand at FAMSI called "Directions and Partitions in Maya World View". See www.famsi.org/research/hopkins/directions.html.

However, there is no substitute for actual first hand witness and I do count it as a major learning experience to have seen these rituals and even participated in them. They ring true to their cultural roots with no reference or apologies to the veneer of Catholic religion that was imposed by the Spanish. As a Wiccan priestess myself, I appreciated the use and meaning of symbols in these rituals and the activation and movement of energy that was created. I am grateful to the modern Maya shamans and their people who are willing to let foreigners peek into this most sacred and intimate part of their lives.

Catalog of Copan Notes

"The Copan Notes are a running series of commentaries and small reports deriving from the multidiscipilary research project designed to conserve, document, and analyze the architectural and sculpture monuments of the Classic Maya ruins of Copan. Originally undertaken by William L. Fash and known as the Copan Mosaics Project, this endeavor has since June of 1988 formed part of the larger Copan Acropolis Project. These projects were funded in part by the Instituto Hondureno de Antropologia e Historia through financing from the U. S. Agency for International Development." This is the statement that accompanies each Copan Note. The statement goes on to list other funding sources and authorizations needed to use material contained in these notes.

There are 121 Copan Notes (numbers 9 and 10 were never completed). They are presently individually in the hands of researchers all over the world, but one of the few places where they are present *in toto* is reportedly at the University of Texas in Austin. The Copan Notes contain a treasure trove of Maya texts and analysis that are difficult to find elsewhere. These are currently not readily accessible. The purpose of this catalog is to identify the titles of the Copan Notes and the illustrations contained in each one. Hopefully when they become available on line, this catalog will be a helpful tool for researchers seeking specific texts.

There is another collection at the same university called Texas Notes on Precolumbian Art, Writing, and Culture which is very accessible on line. The Texas Notes are of the same scholarly level and general format as the Copan Notes but cover the broader Mesoamerican scope.

The list below identifies the Copan Notes by number and the illustrations that can be found in each. In some cases the complete text of a certain monument is illustrated and in others, only an example or portion of the text is illustrated.

The Copan Notes

1. Te-Tun as the Glyph for "Stela"
   - *Copan: stelae C, F, B examples*
   - *Examples from Dresden Codex, Tonina M30 & M74, Palenque sarcophagus*
2. A Glyph for "Stone Incensario"
   - *Copan: CPN 277, 240, 282, 246, 249, 239, 884, 1016, 2a, 3b, ?6a*
3. The Chronology of Altar U
   - *Copan: altar U complete text*
4. The Hieroglypic Name for Altar U
   - *Copan: altar U face plus text*
5. Paraphrase of the Text of Altar U
   - *Copan: altar U complete text*
6. Yax Kuk Mo, Founder of the Lineage of Copan
   - *Copan: altar Q name glyphs*
   - *Copan: stelae B, 15, P, 19, and temple 11reviewing stand succession statements*
7. The "First Ruler" on Stela 24
   - *Copan: stela 24 fragments*
8. The Founders of Lineages at Copan and other Maya sites
   - *Copan: altar Q name glyphs*

- *Copan: stelae 15, P, 7, 19, 13, N, 12, 10, 6, B, E, 24, and temple 11reviewing stand succession statements*
- *Yaxchitlan: lintel 21and other examples*
- *Tikal: stelae 5, 22, 17, 12, 31, 39, monuments 195, 140, and a looted pot examples*
- *Naranjo: stela 24, altar 1 examples*
- *Quirigua: stela J example*

9. Substitution in the Emblem Glyph of Copan (never completed)
10. The Protagonist of Altar G, U, and T (never completed)
11. Thoughts on the Temple Inscription from Temple 26
    - *Poor quality photocopy of inscription*
12. Chronology of Stela 4 at Copan
    - *Copan: stela 4 complete text*
13. Figures on the Central Marker of Ballcourt AIIB at Copan
    - *Copan: central ballcourt 2b and south marker of ballcourt 2a*
    - *Examples of Hun Ahau, Jaguar God of 9, God of Zero*
14. Butz Chan, the 11th Successor of the Lineage of Yax Kuk Mo
    - *Copan: altar Q name glyphs*
    - *Copan: stelae 7, P complete texts and sections of hieroglyphic stair*
15. Moon Jaguar, the 10th Successor of the Lineage of Yax Kuk Mo
    - *Copan: altar Q name glyphs*
    - *Copan: stela 9 complete text, stela 18 fragments, and sections of hieroglyphic stair*
16. Waterlily Jaguar, the 7th Successor of the Lineage of Yax Kuk Mo
    - *Copan: altar Q name glyphs*

- *Copan: stelae 18 and E complete texts, sections of stelae 15, 16, and sections of hieroglyphic stair*
17. Interim Report on the Hieroglyphic Stair of Structure 26
    - *Copan: many sections of hieroglyphic stair*
18. The step inscription of Temple 22 at Copan
    - *No illustrations*
19. Interim Report on the Iconography of the Architectural Sculpture
    - *Copan: temple 22 outer door*
20. The Brother of Yax Pac
    - *Copan: altars G, T examples, and parentage statements for Yax Pac & brother from altar U and stela 8*
21. U Cit Tok, the Last King of Copan
    - *Copan: altar L, full sides of altar Q, east half of temple 11 bench*
22. The Birth Monument of Butz Chan
    - *Copan: altar Y text and statement from stela P*
23. The Date on the Bench from Structure 9N-32, Sepulturas, Copan
    - *Copan: calendar round from the bench, Chac signs from Altars U, Q,*
    - *Copan: temple 11 reviewing stand and south door east panel*
    - *Brief example from Palenque tablet of 96 glyphs*
24. The Figures on the Legs of the Scribe's Bench
    - *Copan: 9N-82 bench and altar W complete texts*
25. Some Ideas of the Protagonists and Dating of Stela E.
    - *Copan: stela E and its altar, stela 15, both complete texts,*
    - *Quirigua: examples of unials, various examples of head variants for number 2 from other places*
26. A Possible Death Date for Smoke Imix God K

- *Copan: two jades from temple 26 and one from stela 7 caches*
- *Palenque: examples of world tree*

35. The Dedication of Structure 2 and a New Form of the God N Event
    - *Copan: temple 4 dedication steps (Note: Schele identifies both illustrations as temple 4, but the title and the identification of the second illustration says 10L-2. These are two different structures.)*

36. Two Altar Names at Copan
    - *Copan: altars G & S complete texts, examples of na-chan bloodletting expression from various places*
    - *Examples of chihchan serpent on pottery, miscellaneous objects*

37. Notes on the Rio Amarillo Altars
    - *Copan: stela 10 complete text*
    - *Rio Amarillo: altar 1 complete text, fragments of stela 2*

38. New Fits on the North Panel of the West Doorway of Temple 11
    - *Copan: temple 11vVariations on north panel of west doorway, south panel of the east door*

39. The Father of Smoke Shell
    - *Copan: stela N base*

40. Cu-Ix, the Fourth Ruler of Copan and his Monuments
    - *Copan: stela 34 fragment, fragment V, figure and name glyphs from altar Q (figure mislabled "successor 2" when it is really successor 4)*

41. A Venus Title on Copan stela F
    - *Copan: stela F complete text*
    - *Yaxchitlan: stela 18 front, La Corona ballplayer panel, Palenque: example of Venus expressions*
    - *Dresden Codex 58a & b*

42. The Future Marker on a Hand Scattering Verb at Copan

- *Copan: stelae 63, 15, 34, 9, E, 7, 18, 35, 49, 32, 48 complete texts*
- *Copan: stelae 20, 24,50, 25, 22, 60, 53, 16, 17, 26 fragments*
- *Copan: CPN 140 fragment, miscellaneous fragments from Morley*
- *Copan: Papagayo step complete text, temple 11 sub step, examples from hieroglyphic stair*

71. The Glyph of "Hole" and the Skeletal Maw of the Underworld
    - *Copan: temple 11 door & bench, stelae A & 29 examples, black hole black water place examples*
    - *Quirigua: black hole lord statment*

72. Preliminary Commentary on a New Altar from Structure 30
    - *Copan: altar by structure 30 and altar F complete texts, "era" expressions*
    - *Copan: south end of principle group map*

73. Further Comments on Stela 6
    - *Copan: stelae 6 and 11 complete texts*
    - *Yaxchitlan: lintel 25*
    - *Tikal: lintel 1 waxaklajun serpent, examples of other beings evoked*
    - *Tikal: ballcourt marker complete text*

74. A New Fragment from Altar J
    - *Copan: Copan altar J' fragment, stelae P & 7 bicephalic serpent bar expressions*
    - *Hun Uiniac expressions from various places*
    - *Oxlahuntun: stela 1 example*

75. Early Quirigua and the Kings of Copan
    - *Quirigua: monument 26 text*
    - *Yaxchitlan: lintel 25 text*
    - *Copan: Papagayo step complete text, altar Q north side*

- *Copan: table of structures, dates and rulers from Copan*

76. The Dedication Stair of "Ante" Temple
    - *Copan: Ante step complete text, various spellings of Waterlily Jaguar name*
    - *Quirigua: stela T verb example*

77. Brothers and Others: New Insights from the "New" Incensarios
    - *Copan: CPN 22350, 22352, 22379, 22342, 22343, 22351 fragments*
    - *Copan: altar G1 statement of Yahau Chan Ah Bac*
    - *Copan: altar U text*

78. New Fragment from Structure 22-6th at Copan, Honduras
    - *Copan: drain under temple 22 fragment*

79. Some Thoughts on Two Jade Pendants from the Termination Cache of "Ante" Structure at Copan
    - *Copan: jades from Ante temple, stelae 7 & P serpent bar glyphs*

80. Speculations from an Epigrapher on Things Archeological in the Acropolis at Copan
    - *Copan: Mascaron temple west cache*
    - *Los Higos: place name*
    - *Copan: jades from stela 7 and Ante caches*
    - *Quirgua: jades from a cache*
    - *Copan: altar to stela M top, Butz Chan name examples from stelae A & P, steps 6 and 7 from hieroglyphic stair*

81. Loundsbury's Contrived Numbers and Two 8 Eb Dates at Copan
    - *Copan: temple 11 reviewing stand and Ante step complete texts*

82. Two Early Classic Monuments from Copan
    - *Copan: CPN 529 & 584 fragments, Popol Hol name from stela 63*

83. Six-Staired Ballcourts
- *Yaxchitlan: hieroglyphic stair 2-steps 4 & 7, various expressions of "stair"*
- *Seibal: stela 7 front, Wak Ebaal place on El Anonal panel*
- *La Amelia: stela 2 rubbing of front and partial text drawing*

84. A Tentative Identification of the Second Successor of the Copan Dynasty
- *Copan: stela 24 fragment, altar Q west side*
- *Yaxchitlan and Palenque succession statements*

85. A New Interpretation of the Temple 18 Jambs
- *Copan: temple 18 both door jambs*

86. The Glyph for Plaza or Court
- *Yaxchitlan, Palenque, Machaquila examples, quadrifoils from various sites*
- *Copan: stelae A & M statements, nah locations at Copan, temple 18 locations statement*
- *Uaxactun: H-sub-3 cosmogram*

87. Royal Gifts to Subordinate Lords
- *Copan: altar K complete text, "sibling" statement from hieroglyphic stair*
- *Copan: house models from structures 30, 29 & 33*

88. A Suggested Reading Order for the West Side of Stela J (misnamed A)
- *Copan stela: J west face,*
- *Copan: cylinder and Yaxchitlan hieroglyphic stair 2 6 shell in hand expression*
- *Tikal: stela 10 example*
- *Expressions for Venus, GI, and "square nosed beastie" from various places*

89. Commentary on Altar G'
- *Copan: altar G' text, Ya Ku Chac name samples*

90. A Possible Death Statement for 18 Rabbit
- *Copan: hieroglyphic stair statements*

113. The Xukpi Stone: A Newly Discovered Early Classic Inscription from the Copan Acropolis. Part 1
- *No illustrations*

114. The Xukpi Stone: A Newly Discovered Early Classic Inscription from the Copan Acropolis. Part 2
- *Copan: Xukpi stone and temple 11 sub step complete texts, hieroglyphic stair example*
- *Palenque: temple of inscriptions example*
- *Various examples from other texts*

115. The 9.17.0.0.0 Eclipse at Quirigua and Copan
- *Poor photograph of Dresden Codex D52a*
- *Quirigua: stela E text*
- *Copan: temple 11 examples*

116. Who Was Popol Kinich?
- *Copan: altar Q portrait altar A' text, stelae 20 and 16 texts*

117. The Floor Marker from Motmot
- *Copan: Motmot floor marker and expanded text, stela J examples*

118. The Texts of Group 10L-2
- *Copan: altar F' complete text (twice), CPN 19649 fragment, text of round altar next to 10L-30*

119. The Founder of Quirigua, Tutum Yol Kinich
- *Quirigua: stela C text and face, stela A face, complete zoomorph B, cartouches from zoomorph P*
- *Quirigua: stela U text*

120. The Text in Temple 21a
- *Copan: temple 21a complete text*

121. The Tikal-Copan Connection. Version 1
- *Bejucal: stela 1 text*
- *Rio Azul: two celts and two earflares with texts*
- *Tikal: stela 3 example*
- *Copan: stela 20 text*
- *Caracol: stela 16 text*
- *Uxbenka stela 1 face*

Afterword

Besides the Copan Notes and the references listed in the bibliographies, there are several other important resources for continued research of the ancient Maya world. The Foundation for the Advancement of Mesoamerican Studies, Inc. (FAMSI at www.famsi.org) is primary. This website links to the PARI Journal, the Mesoweb, the Justin Kerr and Linda Schele databases, research papers, Mayan dictionaries, and much more. In addition, FAMSI offers a daily update service connecting archeologists around the world for breaking news and asking for help.

The Institute for Maya Studies is another valuable resource for research. IMS (www.instituteformayastudies.org) publishes a monthly newsletter that pricks the interest in a variety of directions. I am also very grateful for the generous encouragement and insights offered by Ricardo Agurcia and the Asociacion Copan.

There is no substitute in my mind for primary sources and first hand experience. I have visited many of the Maya sites and Copan in particular many times. I look forward to continued work in the exciting and interesting field of Maya archeology.

www.ingramcontent.com/pod-product-compliance
Lightning Source LLC
Chambersburg PA
CBHW060150300526
45790CB00014B/399